"This is THE book that many of us have been waiting for! With its rigor and empirical illustrations this book is a must read for any scholar interested in putting Bourdieu to work in the field of media and communication research. It usefully and impressively unfolds how Bourdieu's key theoretical concepts can be operationalized into research practice with particular attention to correspondence analysis and is thus a really important contribution in the establishment of field theory as the new paradigm for media studies."

Jannie Møller Hartley,
Professor of Journalism, Roskilde University.

"This is a most timely book. It includes a comprehensive review of Bourdieusian media studies, a pedagogical introduction to Bourdieu's sociology, a convincing demonstration of its applicability in practical research and even an update on how this approach can grasp our digital age. Simply impressive!"

Annick Prieur,
Professor of Sociology, Aalborg University.

"In this excellent one-of-a-kind book, Johan Lindell clearly explains and demonstrates how to put Bourdieu's complete toolkit to work for systematic empirical research. Essential reading for anyone investigating power and inequality in contemporary digital media environments."

Rodney Benson,
Professor of Media, Culture and Communication,
and Sociology, New York University.

I0123696

Bourdieusian Media Studies

Bourdieusian Media Studies illustrates the merits of Pierre Bourdieu's cultural sociological approach in the field of media studies, explicating exactly what a "Bourdieusian" analysis of media would entail, and what new understandings of the digital media landscape would emerge from such an analysis.

The author applies the Bourdieusian concepts of social field, capital, and habitus to understand the social conditions of media and cultural production, media users' practices and preferences, and the power dynamics entailed in social media networks. Based on a careful illumination of Bourdieu's concepts, epistemological assumptions, and methodological approach, the book presents a range of case studies covering television production, the field of media studies itself, media use, and social media networks.

Illustrating the craft of Bourdieusian media studies and shedding new light on key dynamics of digital media culture, this book will appeal to scholars and students working in media studies, media theory, sociology of media, digital media, and cultural production.

Johan Lindell is Associate Professor of Media and Communication Studies at the Department of Informatics and Media, Uppsala University. He has published widely on Bourdieu. His research deals with social inequality and media use, fields of media and cultural production, and the Nordic media system.

Routledge Focus on Media and Cultural Studies

Cultural Chauvinism
Intercultural Communication and the Politics of Superiority
Minabere Ibelema

Crowdfunding and Independence in Film and Music
Blanka Brzozowska and Patryk Galuszka

Building Communities of Trust
Creative Work for Social Change
Ann E. Feldman

Secrecy in Public Relations, Mediation and News Cultures
The Shadow World of the Media Sphere
Anne Cronin

Spanish Horror Film and Television in the 21st Century
Vicente Rodríguez Ortega and Rubén Romero Santos

Gender-Based Violence and Digital Media in South Africa
Millie Phiri

The Politics of Media Scarcity
Greg Elmer and Stephen J. Neville

Spanish Film Policies and Gender
Fernández Meneses

Bourdieusian Media Studies
Johan Lindell

For more information about this series, please visit: www.routledge.com

Bourdieusian Media Studies

Johan Lindell

R Routledge
Taylor & Francis Group

LONDON AND NEW YORK

First published 2025
by Routledge
4 Park Square, Milton Park, Abingdon, Oxon OX14 4RN

and by Routledge
605 Third Avenue, New York, NY 10158

Routledge is an imprint of the Taylor & Francis Group, an informa business

© 2025 Johan Lindell

British Library Cataloguing-in-Publication Data
A catalogue record for this book is available from the British Library

Library of Congress Cataloging-in-Publication Data
Names: Lindell, Johan, author.
Title: Bourdieusian media studies / Johan Lindell.
Description: London ; New York : Routledge, 2024. |
Series: Routledge focus on media and cultural studies | Includes
bibliographical references and index.
Identifiers: LCCN 2024015085 (print) | LCCN 2024015086 (ebook) |
ISBN 9781032421179 (hardback) | ISBN 9781032427775 (paperback) |
ISBN 9781003364245 (ebook)
Subjects: LCSH: Bourdieu, Pierre, 1930-2002. | Mass media—Social aspects. |
Mass media and culture.
Classification: LCC HM479.B68 L56 2024 (print) | LCC HM479.B68
(ebook) | DDC 302.23—dc23/eng/20240523
LC record available at https://lccn.loc.gov/2024015085
LC ebook record available at https://lccn.loc.gov/2024015086

ISBN: 978-1-032-42117-9 (hbk)
ISBN: 978-1-032-42777-5 (pbk)
ISBN: 978-1-003-36424-5 (ebk)

DOI: 10.4324/9781003364245

Typeset in Times New Roman
by codeMantra

This book is dedicated to Majken

Contents

Acknowledgments

During the last decade I have turned to the works of Pierre Bourdieu to explore inequalities in news consumption, television preferences, smartphone uses, and other media practices, but also to study the hierarchies within the social microcosms in which media and cultural production take place. In this book, I synthesize my previous work within the Bourdieusian tradition in an attempt to spell out the epistemological and methodological implications of Bourdieu's understanding of the social world when applied to research questions posed within media and communication studies.

Bourdieu was introduced to British cultural studies in a special issue of *Media, Culture & Society* 45 years ago (Garnham & Williams, 1980). Twenty-five years ago, Benson (1999) introduced Bourdieu to media studies at large, and six years later, Benson and Neveu (2005) presented the French sociologist to journalism studies. In addition, a number of introductions, commentaries, and overviews of Bourdieu's work have appeared in our field, each with its own twist (e.g., Neveu, 2007; Park, 2014; Lindell, 2015; Austin, 2016; Ignatow & Robinson, 2017). While there is no shortage of conceptual overviews, an introduction to Bourdieu's theoretical-methodological research program is still missing. Few media scholars outside of France rely on the method of correspondence analysis – the method that allows (but does not guarantee) translating Bourdieusian conceptualization into Bourdieusian research (Slaatta, 2016). In addressing this gap, the aim of this book is to present the main contours of the research program offered by Bourdieu to the field of media and communication studies. My hope is that this book can serve as a starting point for students and scholars of media and communications who set out to conduct Bourdieusian media studies in ways that comply with the logics of Bourdieu's vision on how to "do" social science. It is my conviction that doing so allows addressing important topics of our time, including questions on dynamics of both change and stability in media and cultural production and social inequalities in media use.

Over the years I have had the pleasure to work together with great colleagues. I would like to thank Stina Bengtsson, Martin Danielsson, Karin Fast, Jan Fredrik Hovden, Peter Jakobsson, André Jansson, Paola Sartoretto, and

Fredrik Stiernstedt for collaborations in various "Bourdieusian media studies".
I would also like to thank Zofie Basta for proofreading two chapter drafts, Laura
Machat-From for the final proofreading, and Stuti Goel as well as Suzanne
Richardson at Routledge for editorial guidance throughout the work on this
book. Special thanks go to Lennart Rosenlund at the University of Stavanger
and Claes Thorén at Uppsala University, who provided valuable input on early
drafts. Any remaining mistakes and blunders are, of course, my own.

This book is based on data collected over the course of the last decade
with the generous support from the Ander Foundation for Media Research
(Anne-Marie och Gustaf Anders Stiftelse för mediaforskning). The book syn-
thesizes, builds upon, and extends arguments and analyses of the following
papers:

Lindell, J. (2015). Bourdieusian media studies: Returning social theory
to old and new media. *Distinktion: Scandinavian Journal of Social Theory*,
16(3), 362–377.

Lindell, J. (2017). Bringing field theory to social media, and vice-versa:
Network-crawling an economy of recognition on Facebook. *Social Media +
Society*, *3*(4), 2056305117735752.

Lindell, J. (2018). *Distinction* recapped: Digital news repertoires in the
class structure. *New Media & Society*, *20*(8), 3029–3049.

Lindell, J. (2020). Establishment versus newcomers, critical versus administrative? Sketching the structure of the Swedish field of media and communication studies. *Nordicom Review*, *41*(2), 109–125.

Lindell, J. (2022). Symbolic violence and the social space: Self-imposing
the mark of disgrace? *Cultural Sociology*, *16*(3), 379–401.

Lindell, J. (2024). Pierre Bourdieu's (1979) *Distinction*. In S. Bengtsson, S. Ericson, & F. Stiernstedt (Eds.), *Media classics*. 242–255, London:
Routledge.

Lindell, J., Jakobsson, P., & Stiernstedt, F. (2020). The field of television
production: Genesis, structure and position-takings. *Poetics*, *80*, 101432.

Lindell, J., Jansson, A., & Fast, K. (2022). I'm here! Conspicuous geomedia practices and the reproduction of social positions on social media. *Information, Communication & Society*, *25*(14), 2063–2082.

Uppsala, in March 2024
Johan Lindell

References

Austin, G. (Ed.). (2016). *New uses of Bourdieu in film and media studies*. New York,
Oxford: Berghahn Books.
Benson, R. (1999). Field theory in comparative context: A new paradigm for media
studies. *Theory and Society*, *28*(3), 463–498.
Benson, R., & Neveu, E. (Eds.). (2005). *Bourdieu and the journalistic field*. Cambridge:
Polity.

Garnham, N., & Williams, R. (1980). Pierre Bourdieu and the sociology of culture: An introduction. *Media, Culture & Society, 2*(3), 209–223.

Ignatow, G., & Robinson, L. (2017). Pierre Bourdieu: Theorizing the digital. *Information, Communication & Society, 20*(7), 950–966.

Lindell, J. (2015). Bourdieusian media studies: Returning social theory to old and new media. *Distinktion: Scandinavian Journal of Social Theory, 16*(3), 362–377.

Neveu, E. (2007). Pierre Bourdieu: Sociologist of media, or sociologist for media scholars? *Journalism Studies, 8*(2), 335–347.

Park, D. W. (2014). *Pierre Bourdieu: A critical introduction to media and communication theory.* New York: Peter Lang.

Slaatta, T. (2016). Micro vs. macro: A reflection on the potentials of field analysis. In C. Paterson, D. Lee, A. Saha, & A. Zoellner (Eds.), *Advancing media production research: Shifting sites, methods, and politics* (pp. 95–111). London: Palgrave Macmillan UK.

1 Introduction

Why Bourdieusian media studies?

Introduction

Pierre Bourdieu (1930–2002) began his academic career as a philosopher, but he conducted his first significant empirical studies as an ethnographer in Algeria during the 1950s. He was appointed Professor of Sociology at the Collège de France in 1981, where he remained until his passing in 2002. During his life Bourdieu developed a distinct theoretical-methodological program, commonly referred to as *field theory*.[1] This approach includes a vast array of concepts, including the field–capital–habitus triptych as well as correspondence analysis (a method developed by French statistician Jean-Paul Benzécri in the 1960s). Field theory has been applied by Bourdieu and his followers to understand culture, norms, and practices in a range of relatively autonomous social microcosms (fields) in society. Such studies include the academic field in *Homo Academicus* (Bourdieu, 1988), elite students and universities in *The State Nobility* (Bourdieu, 1996a), cultural production in *The Rules of Art* (Bourdieu, 1996b), and journalism in *On Television* (Bourdieu, 1998). The program has also been applied to understand the symbolic dimensions of power and social inequality, boundary drawing, and distinctions made by actors across society at large (the social space), primarily in *Distinction* (Bourdieu, 1984).

Given its broad focus, it is no surprise that Bourdieu's work reaches well beyond sociology; his approach occupies a significant position in human geography, organization studies, pedagogy and education, political science, tourism studies, cultural studies, and media and communications. In supplementing other works on Bourdieu, particularly introductions of Bourdieu to the field of media and communication studies, this book attempts to bridge the "ruinous divide between theory and method" (Bourdieu, 1990: 25). This implies unpacking the epistemological principles of field theory and putting special emphasis on empirical applications of Bourdieu's research program.

DOI: 10.4324/9781003364245-1

Bourdieu in media and communication studies and beyond

Today, Bourdieu's influence reaches deep into media and communication studies. One reason behind the adoption of Bourdieu's field theory in media and communication studies was the alternative it provided to both materialist-oriented political economy and cultural studies scholars' accounts on everyday resistance and agency, both of which occupied central positions from which media scholars analyzed the social world (Lunt, 2020). Bourdieu's endeavor to merge the categories of structure and agency via the concepts of field, capital, and habitus (which will be explained in the next chapter) seemed a fruitful way to avoid drawbacks in both Marxist analyses of the media industries and notions of cultural autonomy found in much of cultural studies (Lunt, 2020). Mirrored by sociology at large, field theory thus provided a middle ground between the dominant strains in media and communication studies at the time.

Since the 1980s, after Garnham and Williams's (1980) introduction of Bourdieu to readers of the journal *Media, Culture & Society*, Bourdieu has been adopted internationally across a range of sub-fields in media and communication studies. Journalism researchers have relied on the French sociologist to study continuity and change in the journalistic institution. The notion of the field presented journalism scholars with a "new unit of analysis" (Benson & Neveu, 2005: 11), as it comprises the entire universe of news organizations, journalists, and their practices (e.g., Duval, 2005; Hovden, 2008). The use of Bourdieu in journalism studies has increased significantly over the past decades, with a "sudden surge" after 2009 (Maares & Hanusch, 2022: 742). This research accommodates a growing body of work on topics including the boundaries of the journalistic field in an era where "anyone" can produce journalism, the loss of journalistic autonomy in the face of increased import of tech competencies in the production of news (Eldridge, 2017), and media ethnographic studies on journalistic routines (Schultz, 2007).

Audience researchers from a range of specializations and sub-fields have relied on the concepts of cultural capital (various socially recognized symbolic resources), habitus (socially shaped systems of classification and apprehension), and taste to make sense of persisting class inequalities in how people use and relate to various media (e.g., Robinson, 2009; Danielsson, 2014; Bengtsson, 2015; Lindell, 2018). The relatively recent turn to practice theory in audience studies, which emphasizes what people do with media in their everyday lives, draws heavily on Bourdieu (Couldry, 2004; Lunt, 2020). Research on digital inequality concerning the second and third levels of the digital divide – terms that designate disparities in media usage and the gains of such usage – has frequently turned to the concepts of capital and habitus (e.g., Ragnedda, 2018). Analyses of how (digital) media practices are linked to social positions and a multiplicity of resources also reflect Bourdieu's approach (Helsper, 2012). A key takeaway for audience researchers is Bourdieu's focus on the connection between the "material" or "objective" dimensions of social life, such as class positions and access to social resources, and people's "subjective" orientations, that is, lifestyles, tastes, and preferences. In this vein, media use has been understood as embedded in deep-seated social structures and a habitus that is shared by people in similar life conditions.

Field theory also appears in mediatization scholarship as a method to theorize the dissolution of the boundaries between previously relatively separated institutions in society (Hjarvard, 2008), the role of media in shaping lifestyles (Hjarvard, 2013), and the "communicational doxa" that regulate the inclusion in fields (Jansson, 2015). Furthermore, scholars of digital culture and technology have turned to Bourdieu to theorize technology as "crystalized habitus" (Sterne, 2003) or digital habitus (Romele & Rodighiero, 2020) as a way of avoiding techno-centric models associated with the study of technological innovation. Scholars have, furthermore, scrutinized algorithmically curated taste from the perspective of social reproduction (Gaw, 2022; Lundahl, 2022) and studied the contours of social fields by analyzing data scraped off of social media (Lindell, 2017).

On the media production side, Hesmondhalgh (2006) and Benson and Neveu (2005) paved the way for Bourdieusian analyses of large-scale media production. Following this, Bolin (2009) studied the peculiar place of public service media in the field of cultural production, Lindell and colleagues (2020) have studied the field of television production, and Maguire and Matthews (2010) have unpacked the notion of cultural intermediaries in the study of media producers' power to legitimize tastes and cultural goods. A range of works in journalism studies have relied on the notion of the field to study the social conditions of the production of news (e.g., Hovden, 2008; Örnebring et al., 2018). Levina and Arriaga (2014) transposed the Bourdieusian model of the field of cultural production to study "online fields" characterized by user-generated cultural production. In this vein, Mears (2023) uncovered the place of social media content creation in the "field of cultural production".

Bourdieu was skeptical toward textual approaches, particularly of the tendency to make claims beyond the representational realm from close readings of text and discourse. Rather than directing analytical attention to the intricacies of texts, Bourdieu calls for ethnographic accounts, in the broad sense of the term, in order to grasp the function and meaning of discourse and language within social systems (e.g., Bourdieu, 1988, 1991a). Despite certain onto-epistemological tensions between field theory and textual analysis, attempts have been made to reconcile the Bourdieusian approach with various strands of discourse analysis (Myles, 2010; Phelan, 2011; Sayer, 2017) and framing theory (Benson, 2013; Dodd, 2021). Particularly interesting developments in the realm of content/textual analysis are found in the application of computational methods in the study of large datasets, for instance in the study of the shifting "symbols of class" over time (Voyer et al., 2022).

4 *Introduction: why Bourdieusian media studies?*

This outlook on the usage of Bourdieu in the heterogenic field of media and communication studies is far from exhaustive. It nonetheless serves to illustrate the plethora of works that have applied various aspects in Bourdieu's conceptual toolbox to media and communications topics ranging from institutionalized media production and its social dynamics to audience studies and even textual analysis.

At a more general level, great effort has been made to pedagogically unpack the Bourdieusian approach and link it to the concerns and research questions of media and communication scholars. In many ways, these works paved the way for the present take on Bourdieusian media studies. They include Benson's (1999) introduction of field theory to media studies, Benson and Neveu's (2005) *Bourdieu and the Journalistic Field*, and Park's (2014) theoretical introduction. These broader approaches also include efforts to transpose field theory to the study of digital media (Lindell, 2015; Willig et al., 2015; Ignatow & Robinson, 2017; Ragnedda & Ruiu, 2020) and film studies (Austin, 2016).

Numerous publications in the wider social sciences, particularly in sociology, explain Bourdieu's oeuvre more generally (e.g., Atkinson, 2020). Swartz's (1997) *Culture & Power* not only spells out the epistemological presuppositions and operational meanings of Bourdieu's concepts but also provides a detailed biographical account of Bourdieu's life and work. *The Routledge Companion to Bourdieu's Distinction* (Coulangeon & Duval, 2015) and *The Oxford Handbook of Pierre Bourdieu* (Medvetz & Sallaz, 2018) are invaluable resources covering both practical guidelines for empirical research and theoretical clarification and expansion. The pedagogic outline, including the transcripts of student interviews with Bourdieu in *Invitation to Reflexive Sociology*, is another important resource for anyone learning the fundamentals of Bourdieusian sociology (Bourdieu & Wacquant, 1992). Lastly, there are also methodological introductions, for instance Le Roux and Rouanet (2010) and Hjellbrekke (2019), that constitute indispensable guides to explain the foundations of the statistical method that allowed Bourdieu to translate his sociology into concrete research designs: multiple correspondence analysis.

Why another book on Bourdieu?

Bourdieu remains one of the most cited and frequently debated social scientists. Scholars across a range of disciplines are familiar with field theory's main argument and position in relation to other giants in the humanities and social sciences, including Marx, Goffman, Habermas, Butler, Durkheim, Weber, Arendt, and Foucault. Given this impact and the vast array of previous publications on Bourdieu, also within media and communication studies, one may ask what yet another book on the topic of Pierre Bourdieu would add. The aim of this book is to introduce Pierre Bourdieu's *key concepts*, their *epistemological principles*, and their consequences for *research practice* to media researchers in an accessible way. Centrally, then, this book is firmly rooted in the concepts of field theory, but it puts special emphasis on bringing conceptualizations and theory into the domain of empirical work. Most previous major attempts to introduce field theory to media studies have been theoretically oriented, aiming to explain to media researchers the constituents of Bourdieu's theoretical toolkit. Indeed, Bourdieu is oftentimes "misread as a 'theorist'" (Wacquant, 2018: 649). As such, accounts on how Bourdieu's sociological craft can be applied in empirical studies of media and communication are much less common, compared to theoretical explorations.

Although an emerging body of research in media studies employs correspondence analysis outside of France (e.g., Hovden, 2008, 2023; Slaatta, 2016; Lindell, 2018, 2022; Lindell & Hovden, 2018; Hovden & Rosenlund, 2021; Leguina & Downey, 2021; Lindell et al., 2022; Sivertsen, 2023), the principles and underlying rationale of this method in regard to media and communication studies have not sufficiently been explored in book-length formats. For this reason, this book emphasizes the application of the statistical method of correspondence analysis to shed light on questions pertaining to media production as well as media use. Previous guides to correspondence analysis are rather technical in character and without concrete examples linked to research questions relevant in the domain of media and communication studies. In addition to its focus on correspondence analysis, this book also takes initial steps in applying the relational thinking of field theory to social media ecologies and social network analysis (Chapter 6).

This book sets out to prevent atomized readings of Bourdieu's work. All too often in our field, the conceptual triad of field–capital–habitus – originally intended to be applied as a coherent theoretical framework with an auxiliary methodology (Bourdieu & Wacquant, 1992) – is torn apart and the concepts are used in isolation. Think of the countless studies where habitus, cultural capital, or field are deployed without the other corresponding concepts, or where Bourdieusian concepts are merely pasted onto findings instead of being used to construct the research object from the outset (Grenfell, 2018). Herein the broader epistemological framing of the object of study is lost, even implying that research is merely spiced up with "Bourdieu-babble" (Wacquant, 2018: 650). This book stresses the importance of epistemological stringency. It turns to correspondence analysis – the method that Bourdieu argued allowed researchers to think in terms of fields – and pushes researchers into the relational and non-substantialist thinking of field theory (Chapter 3).

It is against this backdrop that I illustrate how Bourdieu's key theoretical concepts can be operationalized in research practice and shed light on pressing questions in the digital media landscape. This book makes two contributions to the existing works applying Bourdieu to media and communication studies. First, it expands the empirical scope of existing Bourdieu-inspired media research to include digital media ecologies, audiences and media users, and the dynamics of fields of cultural production beyond journalism, which is the common object of study for media and journalism scholars using the notion of field. I seek to bridge the tendency of compartmentalization in the application of Bourdieu in our field. For instance, while journalism scholars tend to focus primarily on the notion of a (journalistic) field (Maares & Hanusch, 2022), audience researchers have relied on (cultural) capital, habitus, and taste while leaving out the concepts of field and social space.

Different segments of media and communication studies have used Bourdieu in different ways, and the theoretical approach offered by Bourdieu on the whole remains largely undiscovered in terms of practical application. The second contribution of the book is that it provides an accessible and non-technical introduction to the method favored by Bourdieu: multiple correspondence analysis. I thus invite the reader to step from the conceptual level to uncover how epistemological assumptions and theoretical framing translate into the practice of conducting empirical research.

Due to the fragmented readings and uses of the French sociologist (a critique already raised in 1980 by Garnham and Williams) and a lack of engagement in correspondence analysis on the part of media scholars, field theory has yet to become a "new paradigm for media studies" (Benson, 1999: 463). In its endeavor to carve out what a Bourdieusian "paradigm" implies for empirical work within media and communication studies, this book revolves around one central question: *What does it mean to conduct Bourdieusian media studies?* While this pedagogical question remains at the center of the book, I deploy Bourdieusian media studies onto a range of empirical data to say something meaningful about (1) how media use and media preferences relate to social inequality, (2) the hierarchies and position-takings in fields of media and cultural production, and (3) how the study of digital interactions with social network analysis can supplement our understanding of fields. This implies that my empirical focus is not put on discourse, media content, or text, although the Bourdieusian approach to textual analysis and other qualitative methods are discussed as important supplements to correspondence analysis.

Why should media researchers bother with Bourdieu?

Thus far I have argued that while Bourdieu has left a clear-cut mark on media and communication studies, his theoretical-methodological approach is seldom used to its full extent in our field. While existing literature on Bourdieu has done a great job in introducing his thinking, we still need a book that takes the step from epistemology, theory, and concepts to research practice in the domain of media and communications. The endeavor to provide a practical research guide to Bourdieu's sociology raises a final question for this introductory chapter: What does Bourdieusian media studies offer to media and communication studies? While there are many answers to this question, I shall focus on five main reasons.

Avoiding the many faces of media-centrism

For decades, there have been ongoing complaints and internal discussions within the field of media and communications regarding its "media-centric" tendencies (e.g., Hesmondhalgh & Toynbee, 2008; Couldry, 2012). This debate connects to questions regarding technological determinism (such as Raymond Williams's [2003] critique of Marshall McLuhan) and the early hype around the empowering potentials of the internet, digital media, and artificial intelligence. Blinded by the tendency to project "his [*sic*] theoretical thinking into the heads of acting agents, the researcher presents the world as he [*sic*] thinks it" (Bourdieu, 2000: 51), techno-determinism fails to account for the social conditions in which media and technology are embedded.

The critique of media-centrism also applies to disputes regarding the onto-logical status of discourse and representation where strands of discourse theory give ontological primacy to the text itself. Critics of this particular form of media-centrism question the extent to which close readings of media content, or text in a wider sense, can reveal anything about the role media plays in people's lives, how they make sense of media, and ultimately, what the power of media is (e.g., Lewis, 1991; Couldry, 2004; Breeze, 2011). Bourdieu mirrors these critics by insisting on understanding power dynamics between groups and the unequal allocation of social resources (including linguistic resources) and how they shape how people make sense of their world. The same critique applies to strands of cultural studies characterized by what we may refer to as fandom as scholarship, wherein the scholar-fan dedicates efforts to the metic-ulous description of a particular film, TV-show, or game. With Bourdieu we avoid treating cultural objects as endowed with innate essences and we focus instead on the relations between the social agents and between cultural objects in the space of available lifestyles and practices.

Elements of media-centrism are also present in individualistically focused research that downplays the role of social structures. In audience research, this approach is born out of the inclination to epistemologically position peo-ple as users of media. By contrast, the Bourdieusian view posits people as social agents located in various fields, thus indicating that the practices and preferences of media users should always be understood in relation to broader lifestyles and social positions. Stressing social scientific autonomy and the researcher's role and responsibility in "constructing" the research object, we also move away from "preconstructed" research problems imported from the media industry. For instance, significant efforts within journalism stud-ies overlap with the interests in the journalistic field itself, as key concerns revolve around how to engage audiences and increase media trust as well as the number of paid subscriptions to news (Lindell, forthcoming). In other corners of our field, organizational and corporate communication scholarship oftentimes directly addresses a given "communication problem" that compa-nies face. While such questions might be worthwhile, particularly for external stakeholders, they remain outside the Bourdieusian project, which focuses on promoting a theory of society and understanding social differentiation and its consequences. Evidently, discussions on media-centrism are multifaceted. The label can be attached to studies that put too much explanatory potential in text or in technology, or scholarship that imports research agendas from the media industry (Lindell, forthcoming). What oftentimes unites critics is the view that media-centrism implies ignoring the sociological dynamics that lie at the heart of human existence. In this sense, Couldry favors a "socially oriented media studies" (2012: 8). The Bourdieusian view fits well with the argument that media and communication are embedded in the "broader contexts of social life" (Thompson, 1995: 11) and that media studies needs to be based in a broader theory of society to not "fragment into bits and pieces that can never possibly tell us anything about the relationship of media to society" (Halloran, 1981/ 1995: 41). The approach hinges on the notion of the social agent, a person positioned in a range of mezzo-level social microcosms (fields) with their own peculiarities, rules, logics, and norms, rooted in the wider space of social positions (social space). The social space and the positions that are constituted by the access to various forms of socially valued resources (capital) are impossible to disregard if we set out to understand how people lead their lives and maneuver in the social world (habitus).

Lastly, media-centrism reflects a silo mentality in that researchers put exclusive focus on a singular medium, genre, affordance, or particular aspect in the media landscape. Bourdieusian media studies instead posits that media practices constitute one particular group out of many available practices in the space of lifestyles. While audience studies' relatively recent turn to the study of media repertoires, and the observation that audiences are "inherently cross-media" (Schrøder, 2011), move beyond the silo mentality, Bourdieusian media studies invites researchers to understand media use in relation to broader repertoires of culture consumption. I shall return to this type of conceptualization in the next chapter. For now, it suffices to say that Bourdieu's insistence on the broader power structures in society and individuals' relations and positions in such structures implies that media scholars drawing on Bourdieu's full methodological approach are by definition non-media-centric.

"New" ways of addressing old questions

Media and communication studies have long explored the relationship between social inequality and forms of media use. These studies range from cultural studies' concern with television reception and everyday media practices to political communication scholars' study of political participation and news consumption. The Bourdieusian approach provides tools to shed light on persisting research questions tied to inequality and media use with a methodological orientation relatively new to media and communication studies.

Akin to principal component analysis, correspondence analysis is a statistical tool for uncovering multidimensional patterns in data (of "qualitative" nature, such as preferences, attitudes, or tastes). Media researchers working in the qualitative tradition could supplement their ethnographic toolkit with correspondence analysis to capture the broader social terrains (fields, social space) of media use and production, that is, categories of an ontological status that renders them invisible to the ethnographic eye (Sallaz, 2018). Turning to the quantitative echelons of our field, the dominant approach has been regression analysis. This method forces data into a preconceived, hypothesized model. Correspondence analysis works the other way around, as the model is extracted from an exploratory analysis of the data. This implies that we can (re)turn to classical questions regarding how demographic variables and social class positions are linked to media usage with a relatively fresh and open-ended perspective.

Furthermore, Bourdieu's idea of various forms of material and symbolic capital unpacks the notions of "class" and "socio-economic status", which are often hastily and dutifully included as control variables in regression models. The Bourdieusian approach considers inequality and social class through multidimensional analysis. Importantly, one of Bourdieu's main contributions to sociology, and to class analysis in particular, is the analysis of not only "vertical" social hierarchies (total volume of capital) but also "horizontal" discrepancies between people with different *types* of social resources, primarily cultural capital and economic capital.

Well-researched questions on the formation of media policy regimes and the production of journalism, television, or film can be approached through the notion of field in combination with correspondence analysis. This prompts researchers to study mezzo-level social microcosms rather than individual agents, texts, or organizations.

Analyzing rising social inequality

The third argument in favor of engaging with Bourdieusian media studies concerns the broader socio-political changes of the last four decades. The neoliberal counter-revolution against the social welfare programs introduced widely across Europe following World War II has had a significant impact throughout the world. In some countries and policy regimes inequality is more or less constant, but inequality is rising in more pronounced welfare societies (Jakobsson et al., 2021). This primarily implies the formation of a new class of the super-rich, but also general tax cuts for the middle class and cuts in public funding. This cements and widens class inequalities more broadly (Piketty, 2017). The surge in right-wing populism across the globe is another trend emphasizing increasingly antagonistic relations between social groups.

In this setting, a social theory geared toward understanding both the dynamics of social positions and how inequalities are maintained in "objective" social positions and "subjective" orientations, such as lifestyles and position-takings, is much needed. This is crucial for the social sciences at large, and also for media and communication researchers (Jakobsson et al., 2021). Bourdieu offers a way to approach the interconnection between (increasing) social inequality and the media landscape, which since the 1980s has turned from a low-choice environment characterized by mass consumption to one characterized by seemingly endless choice and personal curation. Field theory has largely been deployed to understand social differentiation and inequality in modern societies, conceptualizing the social resources that tend to shape how people maneuver in the social world. A media researcher concerned with social inequalities – be it in media access and digital divides, media trust, the gratifications sought from watching TV, music tastes, or practices of public connection – has much to gain from the Bourdieusian approach.

Modernity can be viewed as an epoch characterized by social differentiation, implying the emergence of semi-autonomous social fields (such as academia, journalism, and television production) where specific social resources are produced and struggled over. This suggests that contemporary social inequality is per definition multidimensional and cannot be captured by solely studying economic disparities. The concepts of cultural capital, social capital, and field-specific capital allow media researchers to capture not only fine-grained differences between people across the social space (e.g., in a country's population), but also the internal hierarchies within the fields that produce these capitals.

Straddling divides in class analysis

Fourth, media and communication research is influenced by a range of theories devoted to understanding inequality and power. This includes a wide span of approaches ranging from "culturalist" analyses of how class is experienced, performed, or represented to Marxist analyses of the relations between the owning class and the working class (Jakobsson et al., 2021). In the Bourdieusian view, the culturalist strand is crippled by its tendency to bracket the objective conditions in which social agents are embedded. Meanwhile, Marxists fail to account for "subjective" dimensions tied to how social agents apprehend and make sense of the social world (Bourdieu, 1989). This implies that we are encouraged to "zoom out" from the meticulous details pertaining to particular cases, which produce only partial knowledge, and focus on the overarching structure of the social space and other lifestyles. Reversely, the analyses of media power and the political economy of the media industries are confined to the structural realm, such as mapping ownership structures in the media industries or overarching media policy regimes. While such analyses are undoubtedly important, they fail to consider how inequality plays out in everyday practice. By considering the diverse ways in which social groups make sense of the social world and the social origins of such dispositions,

Bourdieusian media studies promotes a middle way between the Marxist and "culturalist" class analysis common in our field.

Not everything is changing all the time

Fifth, a perspective sensitive to both change and continuity is much needed in a field that is intimately connected to a set of study objects prone to rapid development, that is, technologies of communication and their production, reception, and societal consequences. The field of media and communication studies is sometimes too easily swayed by the opportunities and new affordances offered by the latest technology of communication, or the latest buzzword connected to a particular technology or platform. A few decades ago, it was the empowering potentials of the internet that grabbed media scholars' attention. A few years back, significant parts of the field steered its focus toward Twitter (*X* since 2023) and other social media platforms, not least to study the digital spread of "fake news". Today, our field moves swiftly into the new interdisciplinary domains of big data studies, critical data studies, and AI research. While the rapid changes in study objects and research questions indicate that media and communication studies is a dynamic field that is able to respond to contemporary challenges, they carry the risk that overarching theoretical ambitions remain stagnant. While theories have to be revised and there is no doubt that altogether, new concepts and theories are needed to understand new social conditions, there is also value in anchoring inquiries in broader social theory.

Evidently, our field tends to focus on change rather than continuity (Driessens, 2023). Bourdieu nonetheless reminds us that the production of culture, journalism, and discourse, and so on takes place in social fields characterized by stability and inertia. The ways in which people make sense of media and how they communicate are based in social positions and origins that tend to reproduce the conditions of their making. These well-documented tendencies do not, however, mean that there is no room for social change in the Bourdieusian framework. Heilbron and Steinmetz (2018) "challenge the reader to find a single text by Bourdieu where some form of social change is not discussed". For example, *The Rules of Art* revolves around the emergence and changes in the field of cultural production over the course of two centuries. In the midst of its many examples of class reproduction in lifestyles, *Distinction* also makes crucial points about alterations in social agents' capital endowments following movements through the social space over time. Social change at the level of both the field and the individual is thus included in field theory, but the argument and empirical observations stress that social change in most instances comes about slowly, oftentimes at substantial social costs. Bourdieusian studies on the history and trajectory of fields of media production (e.g., journalism or television production) or studies on the embeddedness of media practices in durable social structures are thus crucial in a discipline that is perhaps too easily swayed by the allure of social change and technological innovation.

Which Bourdieu?

Bourdieu's work spans over more than five decades and deals with tribal society, French culture and society, lifestyles and taste, neoliberalism, cultural production, the educational system, academia, the state, and the economy. It is an understatement to say that Bourdieu has many faces. While art historians turn to *The Rules of Art*, which uncovers the cultural *revolution* leading up to the formation of an autonomous field of literature, educational sociologists might know Bourdieu primarily as a scholar of social *reproduction*, who disclosed the ways in which the school system maintains class inequalities. Ethnographers are likely more drawn to Bourdieu the anthropologist and early writings on the Kabyle, rather than the Bourdieu we are confronted with in *Distinction* or *The State Nobility*, both of which are based on multivariate statistical analysis. Journalism scholars are, at least since Benson and Neveu (2005), familiar with Bourdieu the scholar of mezzo-level fields. Linguists and discourse theorists engage in quarrels (Chouliaraki & Fairclough, 1999) with Bourdieu the philosopher of language, whereas critics of neoliberalism find ammunition in Bourdieu's political writings from the 1990s and onwards.

This book deals with Bourdieu the empirically oriented cultural sociologist, who presents to media and communication scholars a rich theoretical and methodological toolkit. This book does not pretend to offer the full picture of the many faces of the French sociologist, political activist, historian, philosopher, and ethnographer. The Bourdieu covered in this volume is the sociologist who put a system of theoretical concepts to use in the empirical study of not only fields of cultural production but also the relationship between social class and lifestyles in society at large. As such, this book posits field theory not so much as a ready-made model or hypothesis to be translated directly into contemporary research questions but rather as a research program that can be put to use in "empirical analyses conducted in situations different from the one I've studied" (Bourdieu, 1991b: 255). The approach taken in many ways mirrors the ways in which Bourdieu has been put to use in contemporary cultural sociology, wherein Bourdieu's program is well-established (e.g., Hovden, 2008; Prieur et al., 2008; Coulangeon & Duval, 2015; Rosenlund, 2015; Flemmen et al., 2018; Lindell et al., 2020).

Outline of the book

The next chapter (Chapter 2) unpacks the Bourdieusian conceptual vocabulary in the context of media and communication studies. Chapter 3 presents the epistemological principles that underpin field theory and illustrates how the theory is put to use with multiple correspondence analysis. Chapters 4 through 6 are empirical chapters that apply field theory in three different domains. Chapter 4 explores the relationship between the space of social positions (social space) and a range of media practices. Chapter 5 focuses on distinct social microcosms and studies the hierarchies and position-takings inside fields of media and cultural production. Chapter 6 shifts focus away from correspondence analysis and details how social network analysis of digital data may supplement field theory in important ways. Finally, Chapter 7 provides a summary of the book and conclusions to be drawn.

Note

1 Bourdieu's social theory is also referred to as a "theory of practice" (see, e.g., editor's introduction to *Language and Symbolic Power* [Bourdieu, 1991a: 2]). In this book I use "field theory" to designate Bourdieu's social theory/research program.

References

Atkinson, W. (2020). *Bourdieu and after: A guide to relational phenomenology*. New York: Routledge.

Austin, G. (Ed.). (2016). *New uses of Bourdieu in film and media studies*. New York, Oxford: Berghahn Books.

Bengtsson, S. (2015). Digital distinctions: Mechanisms of difference in digital media use. *MedieKultur: Journal of Media and Communication Research, 31*(58), 30–48.

Benson, R. (1999). Field theory in comparative context: A new paradigm for media studies. *Theory and Society, 28*(3), 463–498.

Benson, R. (2013). *Shaping immigration news: A French-American comparison*. Cambridge: Cambridge University Press.

Benson, R., & Neveu, E. (Eds.). (2005). *Bourdieu and the journalistic field*. Cambridge: Polity.

Bolin, G. (2009). Symbolic production and value in media industries. *Journal of Cultural Economy, 2*(3), 345–361.

Bourdieu, P. (1984). *Distinction: A social critique of the judgement of taste*. New York: Routledge.

Bourdieu, P. (1988). *Homo academicus*. Cambridge: Polity.

Bourdieu, P. (1989). Social space and symbolic power. *Sociological Theory, 7*(1), 14–25.

Bourdieu, P. (1990). *The logic of practice*. Stanford, CA: Stanford University Press.

Bourdieu, P. (1991a). *Language and symbolic power*. Cambridge: Polity.

Bourdieu, P. (1991b). Meanwhile, I have come to know all the diseases of sociological understanding. In P. Bourdieu, J.-C. Chamboredon, & J.-C. Passeron (Eds.), *The craft of sociology: Epistemological preliminaries* (pp. 247–259). Berlin, New York: Walter de Gruyter.

Bourdieu, P. (1996a). *The state nobility*. Cambridge: Polity.

Bourdieu, P. (1996b). *The rules of art: Genesis and structure of the literary field*. Cambridge: Polity.

Bourdieu, P. (1998). *On television and journalism*. London: Pluto Press.

Bourdieu, P. (2000). *Pascalian meditations*. Cambridge: Polity Press.

Bourdieu, P., & Wacquant, L. (1992). *An invitation to reflexive sociology*. Cambridge: Polity.

Breeze, R. (2011). Critical discourse analysis and its critics. *Pragmatics. Quarterly Publication of the International Pragmatics Association (IPrA), 21*(4), 493–525.

Chouliaraki, L., & Fairclough, N. (1999). *Discourse in late modernity: Rethinking critical discourse analysis.* Edinburgh: Edinburgh University Press.

Coulangeon, P., & Duval, J. (Eds.). (2015). *The Routledge companion to Bourdieu's Distinction.* London, New York: Routledge.

Couldry, N. (2004). Theorising media as practice. *Social Semiotics, 14*(2), 115–132.

Couldry, N. (2012). *Media, society, world: Social theory and digital media practice.* Cambridge: Polity.

Danielsson, M. (2014). *Digitala distinktioner: Klass och kontinuitet i unga mäns vardagliga mediepraktiker.* [Doctoral dissertation, School of Education and Communication, Jönköping University].

Dodd, B. (2021). A feel for the frame: Towards a Bourdieusian frame analysis. *Poetics, 84,* 101482.

Driessens, O. (2023). Not everything is changing: On the relative neglect and meanings of continuity in communication and social change research. *Communication Theory, 33*(1), 32–41.

Duval, J. (2005). Economic journalism in France. In R. Benson & E. Neveu (Eds.), *Bourdieu and the journalistic field* (pp. 135–155). Cambridge: Polity.

Eldridge, S. A., II (2017). *Online journalism from the periphery: Interloper media and the journalistic field.* New York: Routledge.

Flemmen, M., Jarness, V., & Rosenlund, L. (2018). Social space and cultural class divisions: The forms of capital and contemporary lifestyle differentiation. *The British Journal of Sociology, 69*(1), 124–153.

Garnham, N., & Williams, R. (1980). Pierre Bourdieu and the sociology of culture: An introduction. *Media, Culture & Society, 2*(3), 209–223.

Gaw, F. (2022). Algorithmic logics and the construction of cultural taste of the Netflix recommender system. *Media, Culture & Society, 44*(4), 706–725.

Grenfell, M. (2018). Afterword: Reflecting in/on field theory in practice. In J. Albright, D. Hartman, & J. Widin (Eds.), *Bourdieu's field theory and the social sciences* (pp. 269–291). Singapore: Palgrave Macmillan.

Halloran, J. D. (1981/1995). The context of mass communications research. In O. Boyd-Barret & C. Newbold (Eds.), *Approaches to media: A reader* (pp. 33–42). London: Arnold.

Heilbron, J., & Steinmetz, G. (2018). A defense of Bourdieu. *Catalyst, 2*(1), 35–49.

Helsper, E. J. (2012). A corresponding fields model for the links between social and digital exclusion. *Communication Theory, 22*(4), 403–426.

Hesmondhalgh, D. (2006). Bourdieu, the media and cultural production. *Media, Culture & Society, 28*(2), 211–231.

Hesmondhalgh, D., & Toynbee, J. (2008). Why media studies needs better social theory. In D. Hesmondhalgh & J. Toynbe (Eds.), *Media and social theory* (pp. 1–24). London: Routledge.

Hjarvard, S. (2008). The mediatization of society: A theory of the media as agents of social and cultural change. *Nordicom Review, 29*(2), 105–134.

Hjarvard, S. (2013). *The mediatization of culture and society.* London, New York: Routledge.

Hjellbrekke, J. (2019). *Multiple correspondence analysis for the social sciences.* London: Routledge.

Hovden, J. F. (2008). *Profane and sacred: A study of the Norwegian journalistic field.* Bergen: University of Bergen.

Hovden, J. F. (2023). The same everywhere? Exploring structural homologies of national social fields using the case of journalism. *The British Journal of Sociology, 74*(4), 690–710.

Hovden, J. F., & Rosenlund, L. (2021). Class and everyday media use: A case study from Norway. *Nordicom Review, 42*(S3), 129–149.

Ignatow, G., & Robinson, L. (2017). Pierre Bourdieu: Theorizing the digital. *Information, Communication & Society, 20*(7), 950–966.

Jakobsson, P., Lindell, J., & Stiernstedt, F. (2021). Introduction: Class in/and the media: On the importance of class in media and communication studies. *Nordicom Review, 42*(S3), 1–19.

Jansson, A. (2015). Using Bourdieu in critical mediatization research: Communicational doxa and osmotic pressures in the field of UN organizations. *MedieKultur: Journal of Media and Communication Research, 31*(58), 13–29.

Le Roux, B., & Rouanet, H. (2010). *Multiple correspondence analysis*. London: SAGE.

Leguina, A., & Downey, J. (2021). Getting things done: Inequalities, internet use and everyday life. *New Media & Society, 23*(7), 1824–1849.

Levina, N., & Arriaga, M. (2014). Distinction and status production on user-generated content platforms: Using Bourdieu's theory of cultural production to understand social dynamics in online fields. *Information Systems Research, 25*(3), 468–488.

Lewis, J. (1991). *The ideological octopus*. London: Routledge.

Lindell, J. (2015). Bourdieusian media studies: Returning social theory to old and new media. *Distinktion: Scandinavian Journal of Social Theory, 16*(3), 362–377.

Lindell, J. (2017). Bringing field theory to social media, and vice-versa: Network-crawling an economy of recognition on Facebook. *Social Media + Society, 3*(4), 2056305117735752.

Lindell, J. (2018). *Distinction* recapped: Digital news repertoires in the class structure. *New Media & Society, 20*(8), 3029–3049.

Lindell, J. (2022). Symbolic violence and the social space: Self-imposing the mark of disgrace? *Cultural Sociology, 16*(3), 379–401.

Lindell, J. (forthcoming). Digital journalism and "radical audience studies": Toward a cultural sociology of news use. In S. Banjac, D. Cheruiyot, S. Eldridge, & J. Swart (Eds.), *Routledge companion to digital journalism studies* (2nd ed.). London: Routledge.

Lindell, J., & Hovden, J. F. (2018). Distinctions in the media welfare state: Audience fragmentation in post-egalitarian Sweden. *Media, Culture & Society, 40*(5), 639–655.

Lindell, J., Jakobsson, P., & Stiernstedt, F. (2020). The field of television production: Genesis, structure and position-takings. *Poetics, 80*, 101432.

Lindell, J., Jansson, A., & Fast, K. (2022). I'm here! Conspicuous geomedia practices and the reproduction of social positions on social media. *Information, Communication & Society, 25*(14), 2063–2082.

Lundahl, O. (2022). Algorithmic meta-capital: Bourdieusian analysis of social power through algorithms in media consumption. *Information, Communication & Society, 25*(10), 1440–1455.

Lunt, P. (2020). Practicing media—mediating practice| beyond Bourdieu: The interactionist foundations of media practice theory. *International Journal of Communication, 14*, 2946–2963.

Maares, P., & Hanusch, F. (2022). Interpretations of the journalistic field: A systematic analysis of how journalism scholarship appropriates Bourdieusian thought. *Journalism, 23*(4), 736–754.

Maguire, J. S., & Matthews, J. (2010). Cultural intermediaries and the media. *Sociology Compass*, *4*(7), 405–416.

Mears, A. (2023). Bringing Bourdieu to a content farm: Social media production fields and the cultural economy of attention. *Social Media + Society*, e-pub ahead of print.

Medvetz, T., & Sallaz, J. (Eds.). (2018). *The Oxford handbook of Pierre Bourdieu*. Oxford: Oxford University Press.

Myles, J. F. (2010). *Bourdieu, language and the media*. Basingstoke: Palgrave Macmillan.

Örnebring, H., Karlsson, M., Fast, K., & Lindell, J. (2018). The space of journalistic work: A theoretical model. *Communication Theory*, *28*(4), 403–423.

Park, D. W. (2014). *Pierre Bourdieu: A critical introduction to media and communication theory*. New York: Peter Lang.

Phelan, S. (2011). The media as the neoliberalized sediment: Articulating Laclau's discourse theory with Bourdieu's field theory. In L. Dahlberg & S. Phelan (Eds.), *Discourse theory and critical media politics* (pp. 128–153). Basingstoke: Palgrave Macmillan.

Piketty, T. (2017). *Capital in the twenty-first century*. Cambridge: Harvard University Press.

Prieur, A., Rosenlund, L., & Skjott-Larsen, J. (2008). Cultural capital today: A case study from Denmark. *Poetics*, *36*(1), 45–71.

Ragnedda, M. (2018). Conceptualizing digital capital. *Telematics and Informatics*, *35*(8), 2366–2375.

Ragnedda, M., & Ruiu, M. L. (2020). *Digital capital: A Bourdieusian perspective on the digital divide*. Bingley: Emerald Group Publishing.

Robinson, L. (2009). A taste for the necessary: A Bourdieuian approach to digital inequality. *Information, Communication & Society*, *12*(4), 488–507.

Romele, A., & Rodighiero, D. (2020). Digital habitus or personalization without personality. *Journal of Philosophical Studies*, *13*(37), 98–126.

Rosenlund, L. (2015). Working with Distinction: Scandinavian experiences. In P. Coulangeon & J. Duval (Eds.), *The Routledge companion to Bourdieu's Distinction* (pp. 157–186). London, New York: Routledge.

Sallaz, J. J. (2018). Is a Bourdieusian ethnograhy possible? In T. Medvetz & J. J. Sallaz (Eds.), *The Oxford handbook of Pierre Bourdieu* (pp. 481–502). Oxford: Oxford University Press.

Sayer, R. A. (2017). Bourdieu: Ally or foe of discourse analysis? In R. Wodak & B. Forchtner (Eds.), *The Routledge handbook of language and politics* (pp. 109–121). London: Routledge.

Schrøder, K. C. (2011). Audiences are inherently cross-media: Audience studies and the cross-media challenge. *Communication Management Quarterly*, *18*(6), 5–27.

Schultz, I. (2007). The journalistic gut feeling: Journalistic doxa, news habitus and orthodox news values. *Journalism Practice*, *1*(2), 190–207.

Sivertsen, M. F. (2023). Stratified public connections—beyond the taste for news? *Journalism Studies*. Advance online publication.

Slaatta, T. (2016). Micro vs. macro: A reflection on the potentials of field analysis. In C. Paterson, D. Lee, A. Saha, & A. Zoellner (Eds.), *Advancing media production research: Shifting sites, methods, and politics* (pp. 95–111). London: Palgrave Macmillan UK.

Sterne, J. (2003). Bourdieu, technique and technology. *Cultural Studies*, *17*(3–4), 367–389.

Swartz, D. (1997). *Culture and power: The sociology of Pierre Bourdieu*. Chicago: University of Chicago Press.

Thompson, J. B. (1995). *The media and modernity: A social theory of the media*. Stanford, CA: Stanford University Press.

Voyer, A., Kline, Z. D., & Danton, M. (2022). Symbols of class: A computational analysis of class distinction-making through etiquette, 1922–2017. *Poetics, 94*, 101734.

Wacquant, L. (2018). Four transversal principles for putting Bourdieu to work. In T. Medvetz & J. J. Sallaz (Eds.), *The Oxford handbook of Pierre Bourdieu* (pp. 643–653). Oxford: Oxford University Press.

Williams, R. (2003). *Television: Technology and cultural form*. London, New York: Routledge.

Willig, I., Waltorp, K., & Hartley, J. M. (2015). Field theory approaches to new media practices: An introduction and some theoretical considerations. *MedieKultur: Journal of Media and Communication Research, 31*(58), 1–12.

2 Bourdieusian media studies

Key concepts

Introduction

The Bourdieusian approach constitutes a research program in its own right, including a set of concepts and a particular methodological orientation. As a broad sociological approach, this program was not, of course, designed specifically to address questions regarding media and communication. Bourdieu's only book that explicitly focused on media, *On Television* (Bourdieu, 1998), was a relatively short commentary on French television journalism's failure to provide deep analysis and the subsequent negative impact this field had on other fields (not least the academic field). While *Language and Symbolic Power* theorizes communication it falls short in terms of a focus on mediated communication. The rationale underpinning the present book and this chapter is that a media researcher's best tools lie in Bourdieu's broader sociology. The argument is furthermore that it is perfectly possible, and rewarding, to study media and communication from the perspective of field theory (see Chapter 1). With Bourdieu, we may inquire how media practices, including news consumption patterns, cinematic likings, and tastes in music, and so on, are tied to the multidimensional character of social inequality. We can approach media production from a view that places it inside mezzo-level social fields wherein agents in different positions struggle over legitimacy. As media and communication researchers we can, in short, turn to field theory to shed light on a range of topical issues, including social inequality in terms of how people connect to the public sphere (Hovden, 2023; Sivertsen, 2023), the showcasing of lifestyles on social media (Lindell et al., 2022), the role of digital content farms in the field of cultural production (Mears, 2023), and algorithmic social reproduction (Gaw, 2022; Lundahl, 2022).

Bourdieu's work has a notable and growing influence on media and communication studies, particularly for researchers concerned with digital inequality and media use and among scholars interested in the culture, norms, and practices in fields of media production such as journalism (see Chapter 1). A key challenge in putting Bourdieu to work is not losing the overarching epistemological rationale, the interrelations between key theoretical tools, and

DOI: 10.4324/9781003364245-2

the methodology they imply. This, as argued in Chapter 1, constitutes an area for improvement in our field. This chapter lays the foundation for a holistic approach to field theory and introduces the key concepts of the approach. Chapter 3 then applies these to research designs and empirical work within media and communication studies.

Bourdieu's starting point was a dissatisfaction with contemporary social science, so I begin this chapter by briefly covering his position on the overarching currents of thought in the social sciences. We then turn to the main conceptual apparatus of field–capital–habitus and adjacent concepts. After delving into these key concepts, focus is put on the question of what a Bourdieusian study of media production, media texts, and media use entails. Lastly, common critiques of field theory are presented.

In between Scylla and Charybdis

The main part of Bourdieu's career took place during the second half of the 20th century, a period characterized by conflict between different perspectives in the social sciences, which Bourdieu was quick to engage in. In post-war France, the social sciences were largely divided between critically oriented neo-Marxists and positivists (Coulangeon & Duval, 2015) – "the Scylla and Charybdis of sociology" (Bourdieu, 1991a: 250). The Frankfurt school's anti-empiricist critique of mass culture serves as the example of the former, while Paul Lazarsfeld's measurements of the effects of mass communication fall into the latter. The debates and tensions between "critical" and "administrative" research have, of course, been key to the formation and development of media and communication studies, and the oppositions still remain (Lindell, 2020). In several passages Bourdieu explicitly opposes both camps, arguing that he "wanted to produce an empirical sociology that was theoretically grounded, a sociology that could have critical intentions (like every science) but which had to be performed empirically" (Bourdieu, 1991a: 248).

Besides navigating between "theoreticians" and "positivists", Bourdieu also sought to overcome the oppositions between what he referred to as "subjectivism" and "objectivism" (Bourdieu, 1989). While subjectivism focuses on how the social world is experienced and constructed by social agents, objectivism, by contrast, views individuals as products of the historical and social contexts in which they find themselves (Bourdieu, 1989). At the heart of the opposition is the question regarding the degree of human agency and autonomy in relation to social structures. This opposition is reflected in methodology, as subjectivists favor micro-level and qualitatively rich accounts of how social agents apprehend and make sense of the social world, whereas objectivists view society "from above", focusing on social structures or "social facts" (in the Durkheimian sense) located at the supra-individual level

(Bourdieu, 1989). Bourdieu's theory is an epistemological project aimed at overcoming the long-standing social scientific dualism of structure/agency. He argued that "of all the oppositions that artificially divide social science, the most fundamental, and the most ruinous, is the one that is set up between subjectivism and objectivism" (Bourdieu, 1990: 25). In line with the subjectivist approach, Bourdieu held no doubt that agents "construct their vision of the world", but, in tandem with the objectivists, he argued agents do so "under structural constraints" (Bourdieu, 1989: 18).

What this means in practice is that habitus, that is, agents' subjective representations of the social world – their "schemes of perceptions, thoughts, and actions" (Bourdieu, 1990: 54) – tend to reproduce the "objective" conditions under which it was formed. As such, social reproduction, defined as "the reproduction of the structure of the relations of force between the classes" (Bourdieu & Passeron, 1990: 11), occurs via institutional inculcation, adaptation to norms and values of social fields, and the subsequent non-reflexive recognition of "one's place" within a social system (Bourdieu & Passeron, 1990). A key notion here is *symbolic violence*, which stresses how agents accept their place in society or a field by failing to recognize the arbitrary character of social hierarchy and legitimacy, and by tacitly recognizing the norms in a given field. Thus, "objective" dimensions (e.g., positions and social origins) and "subjective" dimensions (individual orientations) must be understood as dialectically intertwined to properly account for the workings of social life (Bourdieu, 1990, 2013; Bourdieu & Wacquant, 1992).

In the last chapter of *Distinction*, Bourdieu quotes the author Karl Kraus to illustrate his own middle-way: "If I have to choose the lesser of two evils, I choose neither" (1984: 466). Bourdieu's sociology aimed to find a way between prevailing epistemological conflicts in the social sciences and mark a path for the social sciences that avoided both positivist measurement of society and the works marked by "scholastic illusions" lacking in systematic empirical grounding (Bourdieu, 1984, 2000). At the same time, he wanted to create a sociology that took into account people's experiences, practices, and understandings of the social world (the subjective realm) as well as the social structures that shape and are shaped by these perceptions (the objective realm). In the next section I focus on Bourdieu's field–capital–habitus, which is key to operationalizing his broader epistemological project. It should be stressed, however, that Bourdieu's disciple and collaborator Loïc Wacquant has recently argued that the triptych is "incomplete and redundant" (Wacquant, 2018: 648), and that it is perfectly possible to conduct Bourdieusian sociology without the compulsive use of field–capital–habitus. In order to provide a holistic presentation of Bourdieu's approach it is, however, necessary to account for the three main ingredients in his sociology. The triptych is, furthermore, essential to research designs based on correspondence analysis (Rosenlund, 2015; see Chapter 3).

Field–capital–habitus

Ultimately, the field–capital–habitus triptych is used to explain practice (life-styles, position-takings, tastes, attitudes, etc.). This is illustrated in the formula "[(habitus) (capital)] + field = practice" (Bourdieu, 1984: 101). Practice takes place inside specific fields, defined by the unequal distribution of social resources, that constitute the objective conditions from which social agents' apprehension of the social world is formed (habitus). Put bluntly, social structures shape practice which, by virtue of being shaped by social structures, tends to reinforce the same structures. Taken at face value, Bourdieu's formula seems to reflect the "objectivist" and mechanistic take on social reproduction that he fiercely opposed, albeit in an indirect way. It must thus be stressed that Bourdieu focuses on tendencies and regularities, and he is careful to repeat that habitus is not a fate or destiny (Bourdieu & Wacquant, 1992: 133).

Field – a multidimensional social space of objective positions

We can define a field as a social world in which specific, often unspoken, rules apply and wherein "players" participate in struggles for positions. Fields, such as the literary field, the journalistic field, or the scientific field, are social microcosms that are governed to some extent by their own logics, and thus are relatively autonomous in relation to one another. The concept was "originally developed in physics as a way to account for interactions between objects that are not in immediate contact with one another" (Mohr et al., 2020: 117). In field analysis we are thus concerned with all agents and institutions that are involved in the same "game". This implies that we deal with mezzo-level dynamics that are at the same time located "above" the level of individual agents or organizations and "below" the level of media systems, political economy, and policy analysis.

Fields are social universes in which agents, endowed with specific habitus and different volumes of field-specific capital, compete over positions in a collectively recognized "game". Positions in fields are set by access to field-specific capital and tend to correspond to certain position-takings: while newcomers and the non-consecrated avantgarde tend to challenge the order of the field, consecrated agents tend to defend it. A field nonetheless exists only insofar as there are agents that recognize the validity of the struggle played out in the field (*illusio*) and share the same tacit presuppositions with other agents in the field (*doxa*) (Bourdieu, 2005: 37). At the same time, fields tend to "provide themselves with agents equipped with the *habitus* needed to make them work" (1990: 67, italics in original).

A key question concerns the relation between a particular field and the field of power – a "set of dominant power relations in society" (Bourdieu, 1993: 14) constituting a meta-field that encompasses all other fields (Bourdieu & Wacquant, 1992). In modern societies, this overarching field tends to be organized along an opposition between economic and cultural poles. Fields oriented toward cultural matters, such as arts and literature, tend to be dominated by fields that revolve around economic stakes (Bourdieu, 1993; 1996). Thus, understanding a field involves grasping the extent to which it is *heteronomous* or *autonomous*. The more autonomous a field is, the "more completely it fulfills its own logic as a field, the more it tends to suspend or reverse the dominant principle of hierarchization" (Bourdieu, 1993: 39). Reversely, the more heteronomous the field, the more it is dominated by the praxes pertaining to other fields.

If a field demarcates a social universe centered on a specific struggle, expertise, and common sense, such as the production of "art for art's sake", "quality journalism", "good television", or "real science", we can view *social space* (or, the space of social positions) as Bourdieu's replacement of the notion of society (see Bourdieu, 1984, 1985, 1989). Bourdieu posits the social space as a multidimensional space in which agents are positioned "according to the overall volume of capital they possess and, in the second dimension, according to the structure of their capital" (1989: 17). The social world is populated by agents endowed with different types and volumes of capital and habitus (Bourdieu, 1985). This view ruptures the layman notion, as well as the idea of "socio-economic status", viewing social hierarchy and stratification through the metaphor of the ladder, describing only *volume* of capital. By taking into account *what* people's social resources consist of, particularly in terms of cultural and economic capital, Bourdieu advances a multidimensional approach to class society. The metaphor of the ladder is replaced with a map, or the *social space*. It follows that classes, or social groups, are to be discovered empirically by identifying clusters of people that share similar social resources (as is done with correspondence analysis in *Distinction* [1984]). Social reproduction in non-oppressive, late-modern societies tends to ensue tacitly, through institutional socialization in, for example, family life and the educational system (Bourdieu & Passeron, 1990) and through habitus, and the lifestyles, practices, and choices it endorses (Bourdieu, 1984). This implies that the structure of the social space reflects the structure of the *space of lifestyles* (the symbolic space) in a given society at a given point in time. Bourdieu's argument is that there is a structural homology between the two spaces (Bourdieu, 1984; see Chapter 3). The concept of social space, in contrast to "field", allows for the understanding of an agent not only as a "player" of a particular "game" but as a social agent in wider society.

A recent debate surrounding the notion of field and social space concerns their scale. While much of Bourdieu's own work revolves around either distinct fields of cultural production in France or French society as a space of social positions, nothing in his work suggests that "fields are necessarily limited to the perimeters of the nation-state" (Sapiro, 2018: 161). However, the nation-state, in Bourdieu's view, holds a monopoly not only over physical violence (Weber's definition) but also over symbolic violence. The nation still constitutes a key perimeter within which fields are formed and exist, not least because of national educational systems ensuring the distribution of cultural capital. It is nonetheless true that globalization and increased transnational communications imply that fields can more readily transcend geographical barriers (Sapiro, 2018). The example of the academic field lies close at hand, as academics from across the world in many respects share doxa (norms, values), illusio (e.g., taking the "game" of academia seriously), and compete over the same field-specific capital (e.g., publishing in the same international, English-language journals, attempting to get accepted to the same conferences, and competing for the same jobs and titles). Another example is found in the increased value of cosmopolitan capital (e.g., international contacts, intercultural competencies, and frames of reference) for social distinction (Lindell, 2018). In setting out to study a field, a researcher has to define the relevant boundaries of the field in question and make sure that what is described as a field is a social microcosm endowed with a collective history, shared norms and values, and a field-specific capital that participants compete over. Defining the contours of a field is no easy task, as it demands careful ethnographic study of how agents apprehend the field's perimeters (see Chapter 5).

Capital – material and symbolic resources that define positions in social spaces

Agents' positions in distinct social fields or in the broader social space are defined by their access to collectively recognized resources, or capitals. In contrast to Marxist analyses that focus on people's positions in the mode of production, wherein the vast majority of the population are wage workers positioned in an antagonistic relationship to the small minority who own the means of production, Bourdieu defines social class position as access to resources that define living conditions that affect life chances and lifestyles. Bourdieu (1986) defines three main types of social resources, or *capitals*.

Economic capital consists of money, bank deposits, funds, and other material assets. *Cultural capital* is one of Bourdieu's most famous concepts and moves social scientific analysis beyond mercantile exchange into the symbolic dimensions of social life. Cultural capital includes symbolic assets that endow their holders with prestige, such as university degrees and various awards and titles. It exists in three forms (Bourdieu, 1986). *Embodied cultural capital* is the knowledge of how to conduct oneself in a "proper" or "correct" manner, or having grown up in "natural" proximity to what is socially recognized as the legitimate culture. *Objectified cultural capital* is the possession of the "right" kinds of cultural goods and the ability to consume these in the "right" way, whereas *institutionalized cultural capital* designates institutionally sanctioned degrees and titles (such as university degrees). *Social capital*, in turn, consists of an individual's network of contacts. *Symbolic capital*, it must be stressed, "is not a separate form of capital but rather what all capital becomes when it is misrecognized as capital" (Bourdieu, 2000: 242). One such example is field-specific capital, which refers to the resources recognized inside particular social microcosms (e.g., journalistic capital in the journalistic field). The multiple social resources affecting the life chances of individuals, and their unequal distribution, imply that "the games of society" are not based on equality of opportunity. The concept of capital, in short, paints the social world as one of accumulation and heredity, a world characterized by social reproduction (Bourdieu, 1986).

Orthodox Bourdieusians have complained about the "comical multiplication" of the concept of capital and have observed that "hardly a month goes by without some scholar proposing new species!" (Wacquant, 2019: 18). The field of media and communications has seen its fair share of introductions of new species of capital, including digital capital (Ragnedda, 2018), techno-capital (Choi et al., 2021), virality capital (Lindblom et al., 2022), algorithmic meta-capital (Lundahl, 2022), and civic capital (Sivertsen & Hartley, 2023). These categories may be useful in specifying new dynamics in terms of what skills, manners, practices, and objects provide advantageous positions in a field or in society at large, and to capture metamorphoses in symbolic resources. Researchers should nonetheless think twice before introducing a new species of capital. One should ask whether a new species of capital is specifying field-specific capital (such as journalistic capital), to what extent it constitutes a sub-category to cultural capital (such as civic capital), and whether it describes a particular lifestyle or a set of practices rather than a social resource in its own right (such as digital capital and techno-capital). In Bourdieu's conception capital, regardless of form, is a relatively scarce socially recognized resource, possessed by an individual, group, or organization, that takes time to accumulate and can be exchanged for other capitals (a process which oftentimes takes significant amounts of time) (Bourdieu, 1986).

Habitus – the socially shaped system of classification

The concepts of field and capital describe *objective* conditions that characterize social life. We now turn to how these conditions relate to the "subjective realm" of agency and practice. Different living conditions and circumstances, varying due to access to capital, constitute environments in which people form attitudes, values, and practices. Children who grow up with well-educated parents in high positions in the labor market tend to have a more extensive "map of opportunities" compared to children growing up in social conditions deprived of capital. This manifests, for instance, in that children of university-educated parents tend to surpass working-class children in educational attainment without having superior cognitive abilities (Bourdieu & Passeron, 1990; Morris et al., 2016). How we maneuver in the social world, what we feel we can and should do, and what we consider good or bad, cannot be understood without considering *objective* conditions and circumstances, such as social conditionings and backgrounds, that is, access to capital. The notion of *habitus* captures this phenomenon. Habitus is the mental structure through which social agents apprehend the world (Bourdieu, 1989: 18). This system of dispositions, or way of orienting oneself in the world, is "the product of the internalization of the structures of that world" (Bourdieu, 1989: 18), and thus an already structured structure (Bourdieu, 1984: 170). As an embodied social history, the habitus guides social agents when acting in the world. These acts, however, always take place in social contexts, be it fields or the wider social space. Habitus is thus *inculcated* (formed through socialization), *structured* (reflecting the conditions of its making), *durable* (inscribed in the body as a pre-reflexive classification scheme not easily modified) and *transposable* (capable of generating a multiplicity of practices and preferences) (Thompson in Bourdieu, 1991b: 12–13).

With the concept of habitus, which should be understood in relation to field and capital (Bourdieu & Wacquant, 1992), Bourdieu's argument is in line with "subjectivism", stressing that people enjoy a certain freedom of action, or agency. Our lives are not predetermined by family background and social position. Working-class children do not always end up in working-class professions, the "quality news" is not exclusively read by affluent people, and museums are not only visited by the well-educated. But in line with "objectivism", Bourdieu emphasizes that the choices we make in life, and our tastes and lifestyles, tend to correspond to our position in society and in other fields (Bourdieu, 2000). Children from working-class backgrounds are overrepresented in vocational education, and readers of the "quality press" and museum visitors have, on average, comparably high levels of cultural capital at their disposal. Thus, Bourdieu emphasized social reproduction and stability over change and upheaval (although accounts of social change are also embedded in his theoretical apparatus).

This section has covered the main conceptual triad in Bourdieu's work: field–capital–habitus. Habitus is the mental structure through which social agents apprehend the world (Bourdieu, 1989: 18), that is, a structur*ing* structure. Fundamentally, this system of dispositions, that is, this way of orienting oneself in the world, is also the "product of the internalization of the structures of that world" (Bourdieu, 1989: 18). Thus, habitus is also a structur*ed* structure (Bourdieu, 1984: 170). As an embodied social history, habitus guides social agents when they act in the world. These acts, however, always take place in social contexts – *fields* and *social space*. Common to the analysis of both of these levels is the careful attention to power and social reproduction. Regardless of scale (e.g., a sub-field in the field of cultural production or the broader space of social positions), *capital* and *habitus* have a fundamental role in defining an agent's position in a given social context. The next three sections turn to the questions of what it means to locate media and communication in these social contexts. We begin by turning to media production.

Bourdieu and media and cultural production

For Bourdieu and other field theorists, modernity is a process of differentiation through which distinct social microcosms, or fields, are formed (Fligstein & McAdam, 2012). As previously stated, fields are semi-autonomous social settings in which agents are invested in a particular struggle for recognition. Fields are endowed with a particular *doxa* (common sense) and *illusio* (investment and belief in the struggle of the field) upon which participants tacitly agree. Fields thus constitute social environments wherein practice takes place within a set of self-evident and unquestioned rules. Journalists, for example, "have their own skills, myths and values" (Neveu, 2007: 338). Fields, furthermore, are populated by individuals who participate in their struggles from different bases. Some agents are equipped with field-specific resources whereas others are not. Fields are shaped by the social history of its agents. The habitus of an individual, formed via upbringing, education, and inculcation in various fields, shapes an agent's understanding of the social world. Access to capital in combination with a particular habitus sets the framework – or the "space of possibles" (Bourdieu, 1993: 64) – from which practices and orientations materialize. At the same time, the norms, values, and practices in a given field shape the habitus of the participants. In relation to the existing body of media production studies, field theory bridges "the gap between social theory and empirical media studies" to reconcile the macro with the micro, and provides a view of a social microcosm as a whole (Willig, 2016: 63; Slaatta, 2016).

To study fields empirically, Bourdieu relied on correspondence analysis (Chapters 3 and 5 will delve into the details of correspondence analysis applied to the study of fields) because it allows for the study of the overlaps, or homologies, between the structure of a field and various position-takings (attitudes, practices). This method presupposes an initial ethnographic understanding of what counts as social resources in a given field. These resources, or capitals, are then operationalized and studied either through surveys or by collecting and quantifying existing data (e.g., from archives or databases). Exploratory statistical analysis is used to tease out the main principles of stratification in the field. Various position-takings, or different subjective orientations that individual participants hold, can then be located and studied within the structure of the field. In these analyses, the concept of habitus serves as the theoretical explanation, mediating between the "objective" dimension (hierarchies in the field and distribution of capitals) and the "subjective" dimension (attitudes and values) (Bourdieu, 1989; Rosenlund, 2015). Since the social structure of a field is inscribed in agents' dispositions, and capital tends to be unequally distributed, the structure of a field tends to be reproduced and remains relatively stable over time.

Bourdieu (1996) delineated two main principles of division in his work on the field of cultural production: first, division according to the volume of field-specific capital of participants, and second, the degree to which a cultural producer is autonomous or heteronomous in relation to various external pressures (e.g., the political field and the market). Similar principles have been shown to govern the Norwegian journalistic field (Hovden, 2008) and the French cinematic field (Duval, 2016). Other media scholars have critically discussed Bourdieu's outline of the structure of the field of cultural production in relation to the contemporary study of media systems and large-scale media production (Hesmondhalgh, 2006), not least public service media, which is not easily placed in Bourdieu's outline (e.g., Bolin, 2004; see Chapter 5).

Bourdieu's outline of the structure of the field of cultural production may be called into question in the study of large-scale media production. However, a key takeaway is that media and cultural production take place inside specific social microcosms in which the structures of positions and position-takings need to be uncovered empirically. From this view, understanding a field of media production such as journalism is thus not simply a matter of discerning patterns of media ownership, as certain instances of political economy would have it (the so-called "*short circuit* effect" [Bourdieu, 1993: 183, italics in original]). Nor is it enough to confine the study of journalism to a particular newsroom (keeping with the example of the journalistic field). Rather, we have to position the field in question in relation to the overarching "field of power" – as a dominant or dominated field – and identifying the degree to which it is autonomous from other fields. This implies a break with both macro-level political economy and micro-level ethnographies of particular organizations or textual analyses of specific journalistic outputs, as we examine both the location of a particular news organization and the individual journalist within the journalistic field (Bourdieu, 2005, 43; Hovden, 2008). It is in this sense Benson refers to the Bourdieusian approach as a way of "mapping the mezzo" (1999: 479) by empirically drawing the contours of a field, with its internal and external struggles. We furthermore unravel the logics of the field in which media production takes place, regarding both the extent to which the field in question enjoys autonomy in relation to other fields and the internal struggles for dominant positions within the field.

A key question regarding the notion of field is presented by the democratization of the means of production of media content. Since Web 2.0, media production increasingly takes place outside of fields of cultural production and the various institutional norms and values that have governed media and cultural production for decades. Bourdieu's (1984) "cultural intermediaries", the taste-keepers of society, are thus no longer exclusively found within the established media industries, as influencers and opinion-leaders on social media can operate without institutional contexts in front of mass audiences. While some might argue that this renders field theory incapable of understanding media production in the digital era, others productively use field theory to study the shifting dynamics of media production. For instance, Craft and colleagues (2016) noted how reader comments on news items reflect existing journalistic norms, and Solaroli (2016) uncovered how established photojournalists tend to migrate to the field of art when faced with competition from citizen photojournalists, as the distinction between art photography and photojournalism has become blurred. Similar dynamics apply to the new tools for live-monitoring audiences, and the gathering, analysis, and presentation of data in the journalistic field (e.g., through AI, prompts, and interactive visualization). This can set in motion a range of social upheavals, such as the import of tech competencies into the journalistic field and the re-arrangement of what counts as capital within it (Lindblom et al., 2022). The extent to which digital media production resides within or outside of the field of cultural production remains, nonetheless, an empirical question that will have to be answered on a case-to-case basis. The key issue here concerns the extent to which influencers, social media content farms, and ordinary internet users abide by the norms of a given field of media production. If they do, they are part of the field. If they do not, we can study non-institutionalized media production in relation to not only positions in the broader social space but also the universe of available lifestyles (the symbolic space).

Bourdieu and textual analysis

This book is not about the study of representation, text, or discourse. Yet, any book on Bourdieu in relation to media and communication studies should spell out his overarching position on linguistics, discourse analysis, and other textual approaches that are part and parcel of media scholars' theoretical and methodological arsenal. It is no surprise that Bourdieu favored "ethnographic" studies, in the broad meaning of the term, implying that his focus is geared toward the study of practices inside particular fields or the broader social space. In the introductory chapter I argued that one of the benefits of Bourdieusian media studies is that it pushes media and communication researchers toward non-media-centric approaches. Bourdieu's assault on the "internalist vision" (2005: 32), that is, content-oriented accounts of discourse and symbolic power, constitutes a critique of media-centrism (Bourdieu, 1991b). The "internalist" perspective (critiqued in *Language and Symbolic Power* [Bourdieu, 1991b]), which Bourdieu finds in interactionism, structural linguistics, as well as in works of Saussure, Austin, Habermas, Chomsky, and Foucault, promotes efforts to investigate the structure of communication, or discourse, itself. The problem when treating language, or media content in our case, as an autonomous object is that one is "condemned to looking within words for the power of words, that is, looking for it where it is not to be found" (Bourdieu, 1991b: 107):

> [T]he submission of a woman to an order from a man doesn't come just from the words he uses or from what she understands them to mean, but from the respective habitus they have acquired through their gendered

upbringings that already pre-dispose the one to defer, acquiesce, serve and appease and the other to command, lead and expect compliance.

(Sayer, 2017: 8)

Textual analysts thus risk placing themselves in the position of "possessing *in actu* the objective meaning of practices" (Bourdieu, 1990: 33, italics in original), as conclusions on practice and meaning-making processes are extrapolated from close readings of text, and the social agent is positioned as a mere outcome of the inner grammar of communication. This involves an epistemological separation of the analyst from the social world, a position from which the former deciphers the workings of the latter without actually engaging with it (Bourdieu, 1990, 1991b). It is by observing this separation between an isolated empirical piece of communication and its "conditions of production and utilization" that Bourdieu ironically refers to linguistics as the *"the most natural of the social sciences"* (1991b: 33, italics in original). In the 1980s, at the time of his *Homo Academicus*, Bourdieu argued that this epistemological preference gained ground in discourse analysis to the extent that it had rendered it an "indefensible form of internal analysis" (1988: xvii). In another paragraph he castigates Foucault, arguing that

> Michel Foucault transfers into the "paradise of ideas", if I may put it this way, the oppositions and antagonisms which are rooted in the relations between the producers and the consumers of cultural works.
>
> (Bourdieu, 1993: 179)

While Bourdieu primarily addressed the question of communication from a perspective deeply dissatisfied with the premises assumed by structural linguistics à la Saussure and its concern with language, speech, and face-to-face communication, these same points of critique apply to "internalist" accounts of communication and texts in the general sense. What goes on in communication, Bourdieu holds, "remains unintelligible as long as one does not take into account the totality of the structure of power relations that is present, yet invisible, in the exchange" (Bourdieu & Wacquant, 1992: 143). Put differently, this means that social context should be incorporated into the analysis rather than being the object of theorization following an "internalist" analysis. In this way, the analysis of speech, for example, becomes not a matter of deconstructing the "formal properties of grammar" (Bourdieu & Wacquant, 1992: 32), but rather an endeavor to unravel how speech is wielded by social agents occupying different positions in a field or in social space, intentionally or unintentionally (through habitus), and how discourse is embedded in habitus and a given field. The power of communication or discourse, thus, stems not from the communication or discourses themselves but "from the fact that they seem to possess *in themselves* the source of a power which in reality resides in the institutional conditions of their production and reception" (1991b: 111, italics in original). Neveu clarifies that for Bourdieu:

> /.../ neither a newspaper nor a photograph nor a novel can be analyzed only by taking apart its codes, however brilliantly. It is necessary to question its reception and its social uses, the social conditions of its existence and production.
>
> (Neveu, 2005: 203)

The field of media and communication studies has also witnessed its fair share of debate on these grounds. While discourse theorists (e.g., Chouliaraki & Fairclough, 1999) have held their ground against the Bourdieusian critique, arguing that language is constitutive of social relations (which Bourdieu wrongfully ignores), Lewis (1991), Couldry (2004), and others have highlighted the limits to textual analysis:

> The question that should be put to textual analysis that purports to tell us how a cultural product "works" in contemporary culture is almost embarrassingly simple: where's the evidence? Without evidence, everything else is pure speculation.
>
> (Lewis in Couldry, 2004: 117)

These debates highlight the affinity between the Bourdieusian approach and certain strands of audience studies and cultural studies and the distance these fields generally have from pure textual analysis. This does not mean, however, that Bourdieusian media studies per definition excludes textual analysis. Bourdieu occasionally devoted himself to the study of discourse (e.g., between teachers and students) (Sayer, 2017), and *The Rules of Art* (Bourdieu, 1996) is, for instance, partially based on the sociological interpretation of mail correspondence between agents in the field of cultural production. The problem here is not so much the act of studying media content, or the internal structures of communication. Indeed, how would media scholars go about scrutinizing how journalists, politicians, corporations, and so on attempt to construct the social world without the tools of discourse analysis, framing, and content analysis? Rather, the problem emerges in the "unjustifiable abstractions" (Bourdieu, 1988: xvi–xvii) about the social effects of communication without the necessary analysis of the social conditions in which a given text exists.

Several scholars have attempted to merge the Bourdieusian view with different forms of textual analysis. While Sayer (2017) encourages discourse theorists to take seriously Bourdieu's work, not least because of the mutual concern with power relations, Myles (2010) puts forward a critique of the ways in which Bourdieu has been accommodated in the field of media and communication, particularly journalism studies. Journalism scholars inspired by Bourdieu tend to focus on the journalistic profession as such and downplay analyses of the linguistic strategies journalists rely on to deploy their symbolic power (Myles, 2010: 29). For Myles, Bourdieu's approach "present[s] a clear explanation of the nature of the social forces that influence language and underlie 'performativity'" (p. 36). Dodd, in turn, showcases how field theory informs framing analysis by allowing the study of the "genesis and social mechanisms underlying framing practices" (Dodd, 2021: 2; see also Benson, 2013). Thus, textual analysis may supplement the Bourdieusian approach on different counts, for instance in the study of how positions in fields are manifested discursively, or in coding data for correspondence analysis (see Chapter 3).

Bourdieu and media use

Today, field theory and correspondence analysis are established perspectives in the study of culture and social stratification (Flemmen, 2013; Savage & Silva, 2013). This body of research is concerned with the relationship between the distribution of social resources in a given society (the social space) and the universe of available cultural practices and preferences (the symbolic space/the space of lifestyles). This research sheds light on structural overlaps between the two spaces in terms of diets (Atkinson & Deeming, 2015), tastes in music (Savage & Gayo, 2011), and broader lifestyle repertoires (Prieur et al., 2008; Hjellbrekke et al., 2015; Flemmen et al., 2017). In media and communication studies, this perspective has guided studies on news consumption (Lindell, 2018), broader media repertoires (Lindell & Hovden, 2018), public connection (Hovden, 2023; Sivertsen, 2023), and internet use (Leguina & Downey, 2021).

In this view, habitus generates schemes of perception and taste for cultural goods (part of a lifestyle) that correspond to the objective position of the habitus. The space of lifestyles is thus situated *homologically* in relation to the space of social positions (Bourdieu, 1984: 170–171). A Bourdieusian study of media use and media practice involves three main epistemological moves in relation to existing approaches to media audiences: (1) we move from understanding people as media users to understanding them as social agents, (2) we move from studying media practices in isolation from other cultural practices to including broader lifestyles in our analyses, and (3) locate media practices and social agents in the social space with the relational methodology of correspondence analysis.

In regard to the first point, the framing of people as media users or audiences comes with certain limitations. The main risk is that we rely on these categories to create an impoverished epistemological prism through which society ultimately consists of "the media" (whatever this category entails in the given research design) and its audiences and users. This approach has consequences for the research questions we deal with and the studies we design, prompting us to bracket social context and wider questions regarding the social functions of cultural practice. Bourdieusian media studies posits an individual as a *social agent*. Social agents are not primarily "media users". They are, above all, members of a society, participants in certain social microcosms or fields, and members of a family (Bourdieu, 1984). Their position in a given social structure, social biography, movements through the educational system, and subsequent participation in various social fields imply that they embody a certain view on the social world, which shape how they relate to various media and their communicative practices. This change of framing positions the media user in a social world that consists of more than various media institutions or communication technologies and their audiences and users. By linking media use to the plethora of activities and aspirations of social agents, this framing acknowledges the complexities of everyday life.

The Bourdieusian view has affinities with long-standing arguments regarding the extent to which media audiences are "active". These manifest in the reservations found in the work of Stuart Hall (1973) and in cultural studies not only against the US-based media effects tradition, but also against the Frankfurt school and critical political economy. In this context, Bourdieusian media studies promotes a middle way between the assumptions of audience behavior derived from the critical analysis of cultural industries and the qualitatively rich accounts of the lived experiences of media users. Focus is put on the interplay between "objective" structures wherein subjective orientations, including media practices and cultural preferences, are formed. Structural tendencies – the inclination of habitus to reproduce the conditions under which it was formed – are uncovered, without mechanically reducing practice to the pure reflection of structural conditions.

In regard to the second point on how media practices are embedded in broader lifestyles, audience studies holds that media users "are inherently cross-media" (Schrøder, 2011: 6). Partially due to digitalization and increased media convergence, the last two decades of audience research have experienced a "repertoire turn", involving the study of "specific combination[s] of contacts with different media and kinds of content" (Hasebrink & Popp, 2006: 384). While the repertoire turn proposes fruitful ways to further understand broader mediated environments, or the repertoires in which media use is embedded, we can take additional steps in contextualizing media use. When Bourdieu (1984) and his followers (see, e.g., Prieur et al., 2008; Flemmen et al., 2017; Lindell, 2018) study media use, they understand it in relation to myriad other lifestyles. Thus, Bourdieusian media studies focuses on how media use fits within people's wider lifestyles and culture repertoires. Needless to say, how these patterns play out in practice is an empirical question. This connects to the third point, which stresses the use of correspondence analysis in uncovering the relationship between (media) practice and fields (see Chapter 3).

In sum, a Bourdieusian study of media use entails studying how media use is embedded in broader lifestyles and repertoires of cultural and political practices – practices that should be understood in relation to the dynamics of social relations in a society. This move may seem odd, as it implies moving away from media researchers' object of study. If we seek to promote a broader understanding of the role that media practices play in society at large, however, then we must acknowledge the need to study the cultural practices that, alongside media, play key roles in people's everyday lives. A key concept for connecting media use to the broader functions of cultural practices is the social space (Bourdieu, 1984). The social space is an open-ended and multidimensional concept aimed at describing the main forces of differentiation in a society and paves the way for the study of how media use links to subordination and domination on a broad scale (e.g., Lindell, 2018; Lindell & Hovden, 2018; Sivertsen, 2023). The concept is particularly useful in an era characterized by rampant social inequality, increased news avoidance, distrust in the media, and polarization (see, e.g., Hovden, 2023).

Criticism

The critiques of Bourdieu are of different kinds and quality. At the overarching level Riley (2017), for instance, argues that the notion of capital(s) produces a confusing and inconsistent notion of social class and that field theory subsequently fails as a macro-sociological theory. Weberians, in turn, have castigated Bourdieusian scholarship for advancing a confused account of class (for them: economic position) and status (for them: honor, prestige) that does not allow falsification (Chan, 2019). Marxists, in turn, hold that Bourdieu's loose and open-ended approach to social class effectively obscures the most acute dimension of class struggle – that between wage labor and capital (Desan, 2013). Feminist scholars have critiqued Bourdieu for insufficiently theorizing gender, both by "taking the perceived body too seriously by attributing female dispositions to women only and masculine dispositions to men only" and by downplaying real violence and physical abuse (beyond symbolic violence and social reproduction) (McCall, 1992: 845). The leading figure in actor-network-theory, Bruno Latour (2005), has suggested dropping a priori conceptions of "the social" altogether and instead pursue social science by "following the actors".

In relation to field theory's status as a macro-sociological "grand" theory, it must be noted that Bourdieu (e.g., 1991a) explicitly denounced such ambitions. The open-ended character of Bourdieu's theory allows an empirically sophisticated analysis of the dynamics of domination and subordination and position-taking in distinct social microcosms and of society at large. By applying field theory empirically in the study of a range of aspects connected to social life, the task is to "refute" or "generalize" (Bourdieu, 1991a: 255). This retorts Chan's (2019) critique on "falsification" in that we are explicitly encouraged to put concepts to use in empirical research. In regard to the class versus status debate, which cannot be solved here (see, e.g., Flemmen et al., 2019), it is worth stressing that Bourdieu focuses on the relationship between objective properties (capitals, positions) and subjective orientations (practices, tastes, lifestyles, position-takings). This implies that "class" does not refer to an occupational category or relative economic affluence but rather a position in a multidimensional social space. "Status", in turn, refers to the effects of the relationship between the social space and the space of lifestyles (the "symbolic space"). Rather than treating class and status as two separate independent variables (in regression analysis), the Bourdieusian approach studies relationships within and between spaces (e.g., the social space and the space of lifestyles, or the structure of a field and the space of position-takings in that field) (Flemmen et al., 2019). Chapter 3 showcases how this view is operationalized through the relational methodology of correspondence analysis. This implies, in response to Marxism, that we are not explicitly concerned with the struggle between labor and capital, but rather with forms of symbolic domination across a range of social fields. Needless to say, both approaches are important.

Another common critique is that Bourdieu promotes a mechanistic sociology positing that practices (lifestyle, taste, etc.) are little more than reflections of social positions (e.g., Jenkins, 1982). In this line of critique, Bourdieu's work is evaluated primarily at the conceptual level and he is held guilty of being the kind of mechanistic "objectivist" he himself criticized. Bourdieu argues that social agents are inclined, through habitus, to make choices that coincide with their position in a field: structures form habitus, which reproduces structures (Jenkins, 1982). We have to again stress that Bourdieu insists on putting concepts to work. In doing so, researchers tend to arrive at the empirical conclusion that the structure of a field or social space *tends to* be maintained by individuals' socially shaped actions and values. Bourdieu repeatedly stressed that habitus is not a destiny or a fate (Bourdieu & Wacquant, 1992: 133). However, Luc Boltanski (Bourdieu's collaborator in *Distinction*) argues that too much explanatory power was placed in the notion of habitus (de Saint Martin, 2015). It is fair to hold that there are other factors beyond (class) habitus that shape our orientation in the social world, not least in media practices – such as age (Glevarec & Cibois, 2021) and gender (de Saint Martin, 2015). As argued in Chapter 4, these factors can be incorporated into Bourdieusian analysis.

Several commentators maintain that the relationship between social class and lifestyles in France in the 1960s and 1970s, and the dynamics inside the French literary or educational fields, do not apply outside of France. Peterson (1992) argued in an influential article about US lifestyles that the traditional "elite arts activities" no longer function as dividers between the culturally initiated class factions and those less well-off. The dominant classes have become cultural omnivores rather than snobs. There are two main issues with how proponents of the so-called omnivore thesis critique Bourdieu. First, they tend to miss the argument on the "aesthetic gaze" through which Bourdieu (1984) portrays the cultural middle class's tendency to appreciate the "beauty" across a variety of ("high" and "low") cultural goods. Cultural omnivorousness is thus embedded in and part of Bourdieu's theory (Lizardo &

Skiles, 2015). Second, critics fail to appreciate that Bourdieu's point was that fields are subject to (slow) transformation over time. Bourdieu was careful to emphasize that an analysis of the social space and the distribution of lifestyles therein only provides a snapshot of the ongoing struggles over the legitimate lifestyle (Bourdieu, 1984: 249). Exactly what constitutes cultural capital or "legitimate" culture will vary across time and space. The same argument applies to the study of social fields. Commentators have suggested that Bourdieu's (1996) outline of the field of cultural production fails to account for dynamics inscribed in contemporary large-scale fields of media production (Hesmondhalgh, 2006). Again, the point is not to fetishize Bourdieu's findings, but to apply field theory to (new) empirical settings. The strength of Bourdieu's conceptual framework and method is found in its openness and emphasis on always exploring what is going on in different fields.

Lastly, many complain over the complexity of Bourdieu's prose. Drawing on philosopher Gaston Bachelard (1884–1962), one of Bourdieu's most important arguments on the practical craft of social science was that it must break with "preconstructed" understandings if it is to succeed in reaching beyond what is taken for granted and produce a sociologically rich understanding of the phenomenon at hand. Such a break may require a "new language" or concepts that risk being perceived as complicated or impenetrable precisely because they break with "naïve realism" (Bourdieu et al., 1991: 33). Another reason for frustration among Bourdieu's readers is that his concepts evolve over time and materialize in different forms across his works. What is, for instance, the difference between cultural capital in its embodied form and habitus? Should socially recognized lifestyles be conceived as practice or (embodied) cultural capital? Do family names of nobility constitute social capital or cultural capital? How does one define the outer limits of a field? The answers to such questions vary across readings, yet Bourdieu was careful to stress that researchers should use his concepts to "construct" the object of study and put these concepts to empirical work. One should thus avoid the "fetishization of concepts", as Bourdieu "constructed theory not as the haughty master, but as the humble servant of empirical inquiry, and he never advanced the one but through developing the other" (Wacquant, 2018: 649).

Conclusion

Field theory offers a middle way between prevailing social scientific paradigms. While the triptych field–capital–habitus does not provide an exhaustive account of Bourdieu's oeuvre, it helps closing in on the core of Bourdieusian sociology and navigate between critical theory and positivism, structure and agency, and subjectivism and objectivism. Importantly, it allows posing questions regarding the social conditions of media and cultural production, discourse and representation, and media use. A Bourdieusian approach to media production implies situating it in mezzo-level social microcosms. The perspective furthermore implicates avoiding the "internalist vision" that fails to account for conditions of production and the reception of communication when studying framing, representation, and discourse. In the study of media use, focus is put both on the location of various media repertoires in the space of lifestyles and on their correspondence to positions in the social space. In Chapter 6, we delve deeper into digital sociology and the ways in which Bourdieu is being applied to theorize and study digital platforms. This chapter has laid the conceptual foundations of Bourdieusian media studies. In the next chapter (Chapter 3) I distill the epistemological principles of field theory and spell out how the Bourdieusian approach is translated into research design.

References

Atkinson, W., & Deeming, C. (2015). Class and cuisine in contemporary Britain: The social space, the space of food and their homology. *The Sociological Review, 63*(4), 876–896.

Benson, R. (1999). Field theory in comparative context: A new paradigm for media studies. *Theory and Society, 28*(3), 463–498.

Benson, R. (2013). *Shaping immigration news: A French-American comparison.* Cambridge: Cambridge University Press.

Bolin, G. (2004). The value of being public service: The shifting of power relations in Swedish television production. *Media, Culture & Society, 26*(2), 277–287.

Bourdieu, P. (1984). *Distinction: A social critique of the judgement of taste.* New York, London: Routledge.

Bourdieu, P. (1985). The social space and the genesis of groups. *Social Science Information, 24*(2), 195–220.

Bourdieu, P. (1986). The forms of capital. In J. G. Richardson (Ed.), *Handbook of theory and research for the sociology of education* (pp. 241–258). New York, Greenwood: Greenwood Press.

Bourdieu, P. (1988). *Homo academicus.* Cambridge: Polity.

Bourdieu, P. (1989). Social space and symbolic power. *Sociological Theory, 7*(1), 14–25.

Bourdieu, P. (1990). *The logic of practice.* Stanford, CA: Stanford University Press.

Bourdieu, P. (1991a). Meanwhile, I have come to know all the diseases of sociological understanding. In P. Bourdieu, J.-C. Chamboredon, & J.-C. Passeron (Eds.), *The craft of sociology: Epistemological preliminaries* (pp. 247–259). Berlin, New York: Walter de Gruyter.

Bourdieu, P. (1991b). *Language and symbolic power.* Cambridge: Polity.

Bourdieu, P. (1993). *The field of cultural production: Essays on art and literature.* Cambridge: Polity.

Bourdieu, P. (1996). *The rules of art: Genesis and structure of the literary field.* Cambridge: Polity.

Bourdieu, P. (1998). *On television and journalism.* London: Pluto Press.

Bourdieu, P. (2000). *Pascalian meditations.* Cambridge: Polity.

Bourdieu, P. (2005). The political field, the social field, and the journalistic field. In R. Benson & E. Neveu (Eds.), *Bourdieu and the journalistic field* (pp. 29–47). Cambridge: Polity.

Bourdieu, P. (2013). Symbolic capital and social classes. *Journal of Classical Sociology, 13*(2), 292–302.

Bourdieu, P., & Passeron, J.-C. (1990). *Reproduction in education, society and culture.* Los Angeles: Sage.

Bourdieu, P., & Wacquant, L. (1992). *An invitation to reflexive sociology.* Cambridge: Polity.

Bourdieu, P., Chamboredon, J.-C., & Passeron, J.-C. (1991). *The craft of sociology: Epistemological preliminaries.* Berlin, New York: Walter de Gruyter.

Chan, T. (2019). Understanding social status: A reply to Flemmen, Jarness and Rosenlund. *The British Journal of Sociology, 70*(3), 867–881.

Choi, J. R., Straubhaar, J., Skouras, M., Park, S., Santillana, M., & Strover, S. (2021). Techno-capital: Theorizing media and information literacy through information technology capabilities. *New Media & Society, 23*(7), 1989–2011.

Chouliaraki, L., & Fairclough, N. (1999). *Discourse in late modernity: Rethinking critical discourse analysis.* Edinburgh: Edinburgh University Press.

Coulangeon, P., & Duval, J. (2015). Introduction. In P. Coulangeon & J. Duval (Eds.), *The Routledge companion to Bourdieu's Distinction* (pp. 1–12). London, New York: Routledge.

Couldry, N. (2004). Theorising media as practice. *Social Semiotics, 14*(2), 115–132.

Craft, S., Vos, T. P., & David Wolfgang, J. (2016). Reader comments as press criticism: Implications for the journalistic field. *Journalism, 17*(6), 677–693.

De Saint Martin, M. (2015). From "Anatomie du gout" to La Distinction: Attempting to construct the social space: Some markers for the history of research. In P. Coulangeon & J. Duval (Eds.), *The Routledge companion to Bourdieu's Distinction* (pp. 15–28). London, New York: Routledge.

Desan, M. H. (2013). Bourdieu, Marx, and capital: A critique of the extension model. *Sociological Theory, 31*(4), 318–342.

Dodd, B. (2021). A feel for the frame: Towards a Bourdieusian frame analysis. *Poetics, 84*, 101482.

Duval, J. (2016). *Le Cinéma au Xxe siècle. Entre loi du marché et règles de l'art.* Paris: CNRS editions.

Flemmen, M. (2013). Putting Bourdieu to work for class analysis: Reflections on some recent contributions. *The British Journal of Sociology, 64*(2), 325–343.

Flemmen, M., Jarness, V., & Rosenlund, L. (2017). Social space and cultural class divisions: The forms of capital and contemporary lifestyle differentiation. *British Journal of Sociology, 69*(1), 124–153.

Flemmen, M., Jarness, V., & Rosenlund, L. (2019). Class and status: On the misconstrual of the conceptual distinction and a neo-Bourdieusian alternative. *The British Journal of Sociology, 70*(3), 816–866.

Fligstein, N., & McAdam, D. (2012). *A theory of fields.* Oxford: Oxford University Press.

Gaw, F. (2022). Algorithmic logics and the construction of cultural taste of the Netflix recommender system. *Media, Culture & Society, 44*(4), 706–725.

Glevarec, H., & Cibois, P. (2021). Structure and historicity of cultural tastes. Uses of multiple correspondence analysis and sociological theory on age: The case of music and movies. *Cultural Sociology, 15*(2), 271–291.

Hall, S. (1973). *Encoding and decoding in television discourse.* Discussion Paper. Birmingham: University of Birmingham.

Hasebrink, U., & Popp, J. (2006). Media repertoires as a result of selective media use: A conceptual approach to the analysis of patterns of exposure. *Communications, 31*, 369–287.

Hesmondhalgh, D. (2006). Bourdieu, the media and cultural production. *Media, Culture & Society*, *28*(2), 211–231.

Hjellbrekke, J., Jarness, V., & Korsnes, O. (2015). Cultural distinctions in an "egalitarian" society. In P. Coulangeon & J. Duval (Eds.), *The Routledge companion to Bourdieu's Distinction* (pp. 187–206). London, New York: Routledge.

Hovden, J. F. (2008). Profane and sacred: A study of the Norwegian journalistic field. [Doctoral Dissertation, University of Bergen].

Hovden, J. F. (2023). Worlds apart. On class structuration of citizens' political and public attention and engagement in an egalitarian society. *European Journal of Cultural and Political Sociology*, *10*(2), 209–232.

Jenkins, R. (1982). Pierre Bourdieu and the reproduction of determinism. *Sociology*, *16*(2), 270–281.

Latour, B. (2005). *Reassembling the social: An introduction to actor-network-theory*. Oxford: Oxford University Press.

Leguina, A., & Downey, J. (2021). Getting things done: Inequalities, internet use and everyday life. *New Media & Society*, *23*(7), 1824–1849.

Lewis, J. (1991). *The ideological octopus*. London: Routledge.

Lindblom, T., Lindell, J., & Gidlund, K. (2022). Digitalizing the journalistic field: Journalists' views on changes in journalistic autonomy, capital and habitus. *Digital Journalism*, 1–20.

Lindell, J. (2018). Distinction recapped: Digital news repertoires in the class structure. *New Media & Society*, *20*(8), 3029–3049.

Lindell, J. (2020). Establishment versus newcomers, critical versus administrative? Sketching the structure of the Swedish field of media and communication studies. *Nordicom Review*, *41*(2), 109–125.

Lindell, J., & Hovden, J. F. (2018). Distinctions in the media welfare state: Audience fragmentation in post-egalitarian Sweden. *Media, Culture & Society*, *40*(5), 639–655.

Lindell, J., Jansson, A., & Fast, K. (2022). I'm here! Conspicuous geomedia practices and the reproduction of social positions on social media. *Information, Communication & Society*, *25*(14), 2063–2082.

Lizardo, O., & Skiles, L. (2015). After omnivourousness: Is Bourdieu still relevant? In L. Hanquinet & M. Savage (Eds.), *Handbook of the sociology of arts and culture* (pp. 90–103). London, New York: Routledge.

Lundahl, O. (2022). Algorithmic meta-capital: Bourdieusian analysis of social power through algorithms in media consumption. *Information, Communication & Society*, *25*(10), 1440–1455.

McCall, L. (1992). Does gender fit? Bourdieu, feminism, and conceptions of social order. *Theory and Society*, *29*(6), 837–867.

Mears, A. (2023). Bringing Bourdieu to a content farm: Social media production fields and the cultural economy of attention. *Social Media + Society*, e-pub ahead of print.

Mohr, J. W., Bail, C.A., Frye, M., Lena, J. C., Lizardo, O., McDonnell, T. E., Mische, A., Tavory, I., Wherry, F. F. (2020). *Measuring culture*. New York: Columbia University Press.

Morris, T., Dorling, D., & Smith, D. (2016). How well can we predict educational outcomes? Examining the roles of cognitive ability and social position in educational attainment. *Contemporary Social Science*, *11*(2–3), 154–168.

Myles, J. F. (2010). *Bourdieu, language and the media*. Basingstoke: Palgrave Macmillan.

Neveu, E. (2005). Bourdieu, the Frankfurt school, and cultural studies: On some mis-understandings. In R. Benson & E. Neveu (Eds.), *Bourdieu and the journalistic field* (pp. 195–213). Cambridge: Polity.

Neveu, E. (2007). Pierre Bourdieu: Sociologist of media, or sociologist for media scholars? *Journalism Studies, 8*(2), 335–347.

Peterson, R. A. (1992). Understanding audience segmentation: From elite and mass to omnivore and univore. *Poetics, 21,* 243–258.

Prieur, A., Rosenlund, L., & Skjott-Larsen, J. (2008). Cultural capital today: A case study from Denmark. *Poetics, 36*(1), 45–71.

Ragnedda, M. (2018). Conceptualizing digital capital. *Telematics and Informatics, 35*(8), 2366–2375.

Riley, D. (2017). Bourdieu's class theory: The academic as revolutionary. *Catalyst, 1*(2), 107–136.

Rosenlund, L. (2015). Working with distinction: Scandinavian experiences. In P. Coulangeon & J. Duval (Eds.), *The Routledge companion to Bourdieu's Distinction* (pp. 157–186). London, New York: Routledge.

Sapiro, G. (2018). Field theory from a transnational perspective. In T. Medvetz & J. J. Sallaz (Eds.), *The Oxford handbook of Pierre Bourdieu* (pp. 161–182). Oxford: Oxford University Press.

Savage, M., & Gayo, M. (2011). Unravelling the omnivore: A field analysis of contemporary musical taste in the United Kingdom. *Poetics, 39*(5), 337–357.

Savage, M., & Silva, E. B. (2013). Field analysis in cultural sociology. *Cultural Sociology, 7*(2), 111–126.

Sayer, R. A. (2017). Bourdieu: Ally or foe of discourse analysis? In R. Wodak & B. Forchtner (Eds.), *The Routledge handbook of language and politics* (pp. 109–121). London: Routledge.

Schrøder, K. C. (2011). Audiences are inherently cross-media: Audience studies and the cross-media challenge. *Communication Management Quarterly, 18*(6), 5–27.

Sivertsen, M. F. (2023). Stratified public connections—beyond the taste for news? *Journalism Studies,* 1–21.

Sivertsen, M. F., & Hartley, J. M. (2023). Stratified citizens: Conceptualizing civic capital in mediatized societies. *Social Media + Society, 9*(3), 1–11.

Slaatta, T. (2016). Micro vs. macro: A reflection on the potentials of field analysis. In C. Paterson, D. Lee, A. Saha, & A. Zoellner (Eds.), *Advancing media production research: Shifting sites, methods, and politics* (pp. 95–111). London: Palgrave Macmillan UK.

Solaroli, M. (2016). The rules of a middle-brow art: Digital production and cultural consecration in the global field of professional photojournalism. *Poetics, 59,* 50–66.

Wacquant, L. (2018). Four transversal principles for putting Bourdieu to work. In T. Medvetz & J. J. Sallaz (Eds.), *The Oxford handbook of Pierre Bourdieu* (pp. 643–653). Oxford: Oxford University Press.

Wacquant, L. (2019). Bourdieu's dyad: On the primacy of social space and symbolic power. In J. Blasius, F. Lebaron, B. Le Roux, & A. Schmitz (Eds.), *Empirical investigations of social space* (pp. 15–21). Cham: Springer International Publishing. Available at: https://doi.org/10.1007/978-3-030-15387-8_2.

Willig, I. (2016). Field theory and media production: A bridge-building strategy. In C. Paterson, D. Lee, A. Saha, & A. Zoellner (Eds.), *Advancing media production research* (pp. 53–67). London: Palgrave Macmillan.

3 The craft of Bourdieusian media studies

Introduction

The previous chapter covered the key epistemological orientations and theoretical concepts pertaining to field theory and their application in the study of the conditions of media and cultural production, textual analysis, and audience research. This chapter takes the step from the conceptual realm into the domain of empirical research and the craft of research designs. The chapter first recapitulates and highlights key epistemological positions and frames these as underlying principles for the empirical work undertaken within Bourdieusian research. We then turn to multiple correspondence analysis (MCA) and the practical work of using theoretical concepts in "constructing the object" of study, be it the social space, the space of lifestyles (such as the space of media use), or a particular social field (such as the journalistic field). Although the chapter discusses the use of qualitative methods and prosopographic data, it primarily deals with survey data analyzed with a form of geometric data analysis (MCA). While one chapter is not nearly enough in terms of covering the "craft" of Bourdieusian sociology – Bourdieu and colleagues dedicated several books to the topic – this chapter nonetheless provides an overview and basic guidelines. The use of social network analysis to study digital data from a Bourdieusian perspective requires theoretical and methodological re-calibration, and for this reason, social network analysis will be covered in Chapter 6.

Principles

In regard to the epistemological principles underlying field theory, we must first establish that it is *relational* rather than substantialist in its outlook on social life: "Relational theorists reject the notion that one can posit discrete, pre-given units such as the individual or society as ultimate starting points of sociological analysis" (Emirbayer, 1997: 287). The substantialist approach, which Bourdieu frequently castigates, holds that "social phenomena have an ascribed, fixed meaning or essence" (Bourdieu in Marzec, 2019: 19). In the

DOI: 10.4324/9781003364245-3

case of class analysis, for instance, a substantialist view posits the working class as constituted by X properties and holding Y political opinions, tastes, and lifestyles. By contrast, Bourdieu goes to great lengths to avoid treating social groups as "classes on paper" or "theoretical classes" (Bourdieu, 1985), favoring the study of the relationships between positions held by agents in a multidimensional social space or field. It follows that classes, or social groups, are to be uncovered empirically.

In terms of the analysis of lifestyles and various cultural goods (such as music genres, news outlets, magazines, television shows, social media profiles, etc.), a substantialist approach would assume that a particular cultural artifact is endowed with certain innate properties (e.g., assumptions on the "quality" of "quality news" that fail to recognize that "the quality of goods [is] itself highly dependent on the quality of the consumer" [Bourdieu in Coulangeon et al., 2015: 119]). As such, substantialism manifests

> when a practice or a pattern of consumption is taken "in and for itself, independently of the universe of substitutable practice" /.../ for example, boxing might be considered to be an intrinsically lower-class sport, characterised as universally "brutal" and "brainless", yet it only derives its contemporary characterisation from its place in the system as a whole (contra, for example, horse riding or yoga), and historical analysis reveals that it has in fact undergone a shift over time, being originally considered a gentlemanly pursuit of the upper class.
>
> (Marzec, 2019: 19)

We thus focus on relations (e.g., in the distribution of capitals in a field or [dis]connections between different cultural goods and lifestyles) rather than essences (Bourdieu, 2000a: 269). Rather than social classes we can speak of social groups, or clusters of people that share similar capital portfolios. By virtue of sharing objective conditions in social life, social agents are located in close proximity to one another in the social space (the structure of domination/subordination). Rather than attaching to certain practices the labels of "high-brow" or "low-brow", we study the relations within the universe of available lifestyles as well as the links between this symbolic space and the space of social positions. This point speaks directly to the fact that field theory is *open-ended* and *empirically* oriented, and thus not hinged upon the conditions under which it was conceived (i.e., in the study of a range of social microcosms, as well as the relationship between social positions and lifestyles, in France between the 1960s and 1990s), which is a common misunderstanding (Peterson, 1992):

> Those who criticize the "French" character of my findings fail to see what is important, which is not the findings but the process through which they are found. "Theories" are research programmes which call not for

"theoretical discussion" but for practical implementation, which refutes or generalizes.

(Bourdieu, 1991: 255)

A key point is thus not to fetishize Bourdieu's findings, but to put his concepts to use and to promote relational understandings of forms of symbolic domination. The Bourdieusian approach is firmly anchored in *empirical analysis* of a given field or social space. We can only fully understand people's media practices and lifestyles, the structure of class relations in a given society, and the hierarchies within social fields when we empirically uncover the relations between properties (such as capitals) in an exploratory manner. Although essentially open-ended, field theory is, at the same time, not some variant of grounded theory or actor-network-theory – both of which attempt to initiate analysis from a theoretically clean slate by, for instance, simply "following the actors" (Latour, 2005). Put together into one epistemic whole, Bourdieu's concepts form an overarching theory of the social world according to which modern societies are differentiated into various social microcosms (fields) wherein social agents equipped with different social resources (capitals) move about (habitus) in ways that often, but not always, maintain the structures of fields.

Empirical work within the Bourdieusian tradition often starts with a set of theoretical concepts, for example, the field–capital–habitus triptych. These concepts are not, however, substantialist in nature. What a field "is", how far in time and space it reaches, and what agents are included in it are open-ended questions that must be answered by way of careful "construction of the object" (Bourdieu, 1991: 248) and empirical research that breaks with "naïve realism" stemming from the social scientist relying on "preconstructed objects" (Bourdieu, 1991: 33). The same holds for the notion of capital. There is, for instance, no pre-set definition within the Bourdieusian approach that would claim that a university diploma constitutes cultural capital, although this is almost always the case in modern and differentiated societies in which the state has institutionalized the production and distribution of cultural capital via the educational system (Bourdieu & Passeron, 1990). Capital becomes capital when it is misrecognized as capital, that is, when social agents ascribe some value to it (Bourdieu, 1986). Habitus and the ways in which it becomes manifest in the relations between objective conditions of existence and subjective orientations in the social world is also subject to empirical scrutiny. In response to critics claiming that Bourdieu puts forward a "mechanistic", and indeed also "substantialist", theory of social reproduction, Bourdieu retorts:

How can one fail to see that the degree to which a habitus is systematic (or, on the contrary, divided and contradictory) and constant (or fluctuating and variable) depends on the social conditions of its formation and exercise, and that this can and must be measured and explained empirically?

(Bourdieu, 2000b: 64)

Despite Bourdieu's insistence on an exploratory and empirical approach to the social world, we must recognize that he does offer an overarching theory of society. This implies that Bourdieu presents something different than the "sociology of variables" or "variable analysis" (Blumer, 1956; Marzec, 2019) found across the social sciences, including media and communication studies. Within a "sociology of variables", theory is used to explain the relationships between a set of independent and dependent variables. In many studies of the antecedents of news consumption, for instance, researchers identify one theory or body of previous studies that would explain why the variable "political interest" positively correlates with news consumption, and an altogether different strand of theory to unravel why women are more likely than men to shy away from news. In this version of social scientific inquiry, focus is put on theorizing and measuring various outcomes, perhaps at the expense of promoting an overarching theory of the social world.

Lastly, as argued in the previous chapter, Bourdieu paves a *middle way* between objectivist approaches holding that "social life must be explained, not by the conception of those who participate in it, but by deep causes that lie outside of consciousness" (Durkheim in Bourdieu, 1989: 15) and subjectivists that "reduce the social world to the representations that agents have of it" (Bourdieu, 1989: 15). Bourdieu's "constructivist structuralism", materialized in the application of the notions of field–capital–habitus in empirical work, allows joining together these seemingly irreconcilable views (Bourdieu, 1989: 14). Bourdieu's approach is objectivist in the sense that it recognizes the molding force of social structures that lie outside of individuals' control (social space, field). It is subjectivist in that it pays careful attention to how social agents move about in and understand the social world (habitus).

The present outline echoes much of Wacquant's four "transversal principles for putting Bourdieu to work" (2018: 645). In the Bachelard moment, Bourdieu breaks with common-sense (oftentimes "substantialist") understandings. In the Weberian moment, we recognize that domination tends to pervade social life, but that it cannot be reduced to economic disparities (cf. cultural capital, field-specific capital). In the Leibnizian-Durkheimian moment, Bourdieu deploys topological reasoning on statistical analysis to uncover correspondences between the symbolic space (the space of lifestyles) and the social space in an open-ended manner. Sociology in this sense is a *social topology*, "an analysis of relative positions and of the objective relations between these positions" (Bourdieu, 1989: 16). Lastly, in the Cassirer moment we recognize the interplay between social structures and the "classificatory schemata through which agents give pattern and meaning to the world" (Wacquant, 2018: 648) (cf. field–capital–habitus).

Given these peculiarities, Bourdieusian media studies set itself apart from established research traditions in media and communication studies (Benson, 1999). Many of the traditions upon which significant parts of media and communication studies were founded have been the targets of Bourdieu's fierce,

and perhaps not always entirely fair, reproach. Vis-à-vis the seemingly dispa-
rate fields of semiotics, rhetoric, discourse analysis, and the Toronto school
(or medium theory), the Bourdieusian view is less focused on the "essence"
of the text, discourse, or technology in itself and more oriented toward the
relations between cultural objects. Marxist-inspired political economy of
the media would, in the Bourdieusian view, be constrained by its objectivist inclination to bracket out both audiences' sensemaking (a critique that
often has come from cultural studies [Grossberg, 1995]) and organizational
dynamics within fields in the media industries. Due to a similar "objectivist"
tendency, field theory is irreconcilable with the critical theory of the Frankfurt school, which ignores "dispositions and perceptual schemes concerning
media messages and cultural works" (Neveu, 2005: 199). Furthermore, the
rational choice epistemology underpinning uses and gratifications research is
fundamentally at odds with the dynamics described by the concept of habitus,
whereas much of the work within the media effects tradition constitutes examples par excellence of a "sociology of variables" as delineated above. Much
research in media and communications takes stock of the performance and
quality of journalism, deliberation in online fora, and the behaviors of media
audiences through the lens of Habermas's (1989) theory of the public sphere.
In Bourdieu's (perhaps somewhat unfair) view, Habermas

> obscures and represses the question of the economic and social condi-
> tions that would have to be fulfilled in order to allow the public delibera-
> tion capable of leading to a rational consensus /.../ How indeed can it be
> ignored that, even within scholastic worlds, cognitive interests are rooted
> in strategic and instrumental social interests, that the force of arguments
> counts for little against the arguments of force (or even against desires,
> needs, passions and, above all, dispositions), and that domination is never
> absent from social relations of communication?

> (Bourdieu, 2000b: 65)

The contrast to yet another influential strand in our field, cultural studies, may
not be as stark, as key works coming out of the Birmingham Centre for Cultural Studies since the 1970s have paved the way for the analysis of how ordinary people make sense of media, and form lifestyles, in ways that consider
broader power relations connected to race, gender, sexuality, and social class.
In fact, Bourdieu facilitated the translation of key works in cultural studies (by
Richard Hoggart, E. P. Thompson, and Paul Willis) (Neveu, 2005). However,
the notions of fields and capitals and their empirical scrutiny through correspondence analysis set the Bourdieusian view apart from its more qualitatively
oriented counterpart that in the 1980s would gradually "slide into postmodern
relativism" (Neveu, 2005: 205). One does not, it should be stressed, have to
share Bourdieu's antagonistic approach to competing paradigms in order to
find in field theory useful tools for studying media use and media production.

This section has recapped some of the key epistemological principles uncovered in the previous chapter. We now turn to how principles of field theory translate into research design.

Principles applied: multiple correspondence analysis

> I make a lot of use of correspondence analysis, because I think it's an essentially relational technique whose philosophy entirely corresponds to what social reality is in my view. It's a technique that "thinks" in terms of relationships, as I try to do with the idea of the field.
>
> (Bourdieu, 1991: 254)

Various correspondence analyses formed the empirical bases of Bourdieu's work, including the analysis of the links between lifestyles and social positions in *Distinction* and the structure of the French university field in *The State Nobility* and *Homo Academicus*. Like many methods in the social sciences, MCA usually starts from a set of survey questions asked to a number of respondents. Alternatively, MCA is used on already existing data, as found in archives, magazines, biographies, databases, and online repositories. This method of data collection, which I shall return to in Chapter 5, is referred to as prosopography and involves studying a "collective biography" (Broady, 2002: 381). Prosopography is primarily used in the study of distinct social fields, such as the literary field (Sapiro, 2002), not least historically.

While based on standard "persons × questions" tables, geometric data analysis (such as MCA) differs from conventional statistical techniques (such as regression analysis). Instead of estimating the effects of a number of independent variables on a dependent variable, MCA lets a number of *active* variables create a multidimensional space visualized as a two-dimensional map. *Supplementary*, or passive, variables and their categories are then projected onto the map, without affecting its structure, and given coordinates based on chi-squared distances (for in-depth introductions to MCA, see, e.g., Greenacre & Blasius, 2006; Le Roux & Rouanet, 2010; Hjellbrekke, 2019). MCA focuses on individuals "in terms of what distinguishes them from one another, of how they deviate from the average" (Duval, 2005: 136). While regression analysis and other commonly used methods prefer normally distributed continuous data, MCA research deals almost exclusively with qualitative variables (e.g., ordinal variables such as levels of education and income, Likert-scaled variables capturing likes and dislikes, or nominal variables such as the choice of a favorite film or other lifestyle manifestations).

Much like factor analysis (e.g., principal component analysis), MCA works in such a way that factors, or dimensions, are extracted from a set of variables. The method summarizes the variation in variables and reduces the complexity of data and is thus able to reveal the "hidden structures" in fields (Duval, 2018: 519). Generally, the researcher seeks to interpret as few dimensions as possible, but one rule of thumb is to include and analyze as many dimensions as needed to account for 80 percent of the inertia (Hjellbrekke, 2019: 18). The dimensions retrieved from MCA must then be subjected to careful analysis, both quantitatively (Which variables and variable categories contribute most to a given dimension?) and qualitatively (What opposition does a given dimension seem to capture?), and the researcher cannot beforehand decide on a model that is being tested: "the model should follow the data, not vice versa" (Benzécri in Rosenlund, 2015: 167).

This, of course, contrasts the thinking in regression analysis, where theoretical models and hypotheses are applied to the data. While based on a general theory of social differentiation, the Bourdieusian use of MCA begins "from below". By operationalizing and exploring the key capitals the method teases out the main differences in a field and provides dimensions that summarize the main oppositions in the data. MCA presents a "cloud of individuals", plotting the included respondents in relation to the retained dimensions, wherein "two individuals are similar to each other if they tend to 'choose' the same values, i.e., categories, across a given set of variables" (Hjellbrekke, 2019: 35). We also get a "cloud of categories", showing the positions of the categories pertaining to the active variables that were used to construct the space:

> Each category point can be described as a mean point, or "local" point of gravitation, for all the individuals who have "chosen" the same categories. If two category points are located in proximity to each other, they tend to "catch" the same individuals.
>
> (Hjellbrekke, 2019: 35)

In the construction of the social space, which I shall return to in a hands-on manner later in this chapter, a number of indicators of economic capital and cultural capital are set as active variables. MCA then retains the latent dimensions from the active variables. After careful interpretation we might find that the first two dimensions account for a significant percent of the inertia, and that they describe capital volume (high/low) and capital composition (cultural capital versus economic capital), respectively (e.g., Flemmen et al., 2018; Lindell & Hovden, 2018; Rosenlund, 2015, 2019). Supplementary variables, such as newspaper preferences, attitudes toward journalism, favorite television shows, social media practices, and so on, can then be projected into the representation of the social space. By studying the distributions of the categories in such supplementary variables, we are allowed to assess the extent to which media preferences and practices are "explained" by the active variables that were used to construct the space. If the position of a supplementary category, for example, daily consumption of *The Guardian*, deviates >.5 from the center of the space, we have a good indication that this particular practice connects well to axes (or dimensions) making up the social space. Reversely, associations <.5 are considered small (Hjellbrekke, 2019: 64). Thus, if a certain lifestyle pattern, such as occasionally reading the online editions of the tabloid papers, is positioned close to the center of an MCA map, this signifies a non-distinctive practice not bound to a particular social group. It should be stressed, however, that relatively small associations can still reveal sociologically interesting patterns, for instance if "demanding" tastes cluster among social groups rich in cultural capital while expensive lifestyles reflect positions of economic affluence (Flemmen et al., 2018). In sum, the position of a supplementary category in the social space reveals its social origin. Distances between points in the statistical space are thus indicative of "social distances" (Bourdieu, 1989: 16).

MCA rhymes well with the epistemological principles outlined in the previous section (and in Chapter 2). The method merges the theoretical thinking of fields with research practice and thus disintegrates what Bourdieu viewed as a "disastrous opposition between theory and method" (Bourdieu, 1991: 254). MCA is *relational* and *topological*, as it analyzes, visualizes, and spatializes relations between different categories among a multitude of variables. It is an *open-ended* method that, in Bourdieu's use of it, insists on having the (theoretical) model develop in tandem with empirical reality. By allowing a focus on the complex interrelations between positions (such as capitals) and dispositions (such as lifestyles, attitudes, practices), the method allows critical inquiries into the relationship between social structures and subjective orientations, and to transcend the "ruinous" divide between objectivism and subjectivism (Bourdieu, 1990: 25).

The affinities between geometric data analysis (in particular MCA) and Bourdieu's field theory do not stem from a "fortuitous encounter" (Lebaron & Le Roux, 2018: 503). Rather, Jean-Paul Benzécri, who was a key figure in the advancement of geometric data analysis (and whom Bourdieu knew from the École Normale Supérieure), developed his statistical approach at the time when Bourdieu formulated the concept of field in the mid-1960s (Lebaron & Le Roux, 2018). As such, the theory of fields was fashioned in tandem with the development of geometric data analysis – a method that strengthened the "implicit philosophy" of field theory (Lebaron & Le Roux, 2018: 503). Vice versa, the impact of Bourdieu's field theory on the social sciences facilitated the spread of geometric data analysis internationally (Lebaron & Le Roux, 2018; Hjellbrekke, 2019).

While Bourdieu helped to pave the way for the spread of MCA, it took decades before the method became known and used among social scientists outside of France (Savage & Silva, 2013; Duval, 2018). Today, however, the international field of Bourdieusian MCA-oriented sociology seems to have matured into a relatively close-knit field (in the Bourdieusian sense) in its own right. Participants in this sub-field of the social sciences, the majority of which are European sociologists, share *doxa* (the conviction that Bourdieu provides the best tools for analyzing the social world), *illusio* (the investment in the struggle over who is Bourdieu's progeny), and *capitals* (the credentials ingrained in possessing the legitimate understanding of Bourdieu and MCA). The struggles in this field manifest in scholarly outlets and discursive battles over the correct use and interpretation of MCA (Atkinson, 2016; Flemmen & Hjellbrekke, 2016). Like with other fields, the internal scuffles may strike an outsider as hair splitting. For the players of the game, however, positions in the field are at stake. Ultimately, this speaks of a relative maturity of the field, and Bourdieusian sociology and the statistical maneuvers taken to shed light on important research questions are progressively improved. This is illustrated, for example, in ambitious attempts to use MCA to study structural change/stability in fields over time (e.g., Ginsburger, 2022; Toft, 2022).

Box 3.1   Software used for MCA

There are different statistical packages available to run MCA. While standard statistical software such as SPSS includes the correspondence analysis function, experts in the field tend to favor SPAD. SPAD is, however, relatively expensive and many educational institutions do not have license agreements in place. Commonly used alternatives are various packages inside the programming language R (an open-source software). The analyses presented throughout this book have been conducted in the R-packages FactoMineR and Soc.ca. A beginner setting out to conduct Bourdieusian empirical research is advised to first get acquainted with the epistemological principles of the Bourdieusian approach to MCA outlined here and elsewhere (Bourdieu & Wacquant, 1992; Duval, 2018; Lebaron & Le Roux, 2018), since "doing correspondence analysis is not enough to do 'analyses à la Bourdieu'" (Rouanet in Hjellbrekke, 2019: xv), and then consult the statistical introductions to MCA (Le Roux & Rouanet, 2010; Hjellbrekke, 2019). In terms of practical guides, the many YouTube tutorials produced by FactoMineR developer François Husson are indispensable resources for the beginner.

Bourdieusian models

I have thus far covered the epistemological principles of field theory and the basic thinking within MCA. In this section, we take some further steps into the realm of operationalization and models for research designs. Figure 3.1 visualizes field theory as put into research practice (Rosenlund, 2015). The figure accommodates two distinct analytical strategies and captures the dialectical thinking in field theory. When Bourdieusian scholars speak of the "objective" realm, "capitals", "positions", and "properties", they describe the left-hand side in Figure 3.1. Conversely, when they talk of "position-takings", "lifestyles", "dispositions", and the "subjective" realm, they move about in the right-hand side the figure. These two domains are interlinked as the social world "exists twice" (Bourdieu, 2013: 296): once in the unequal distribution of social resources (capitals), and once in the ways in which social agents apprehend and classify the social world via habitus.

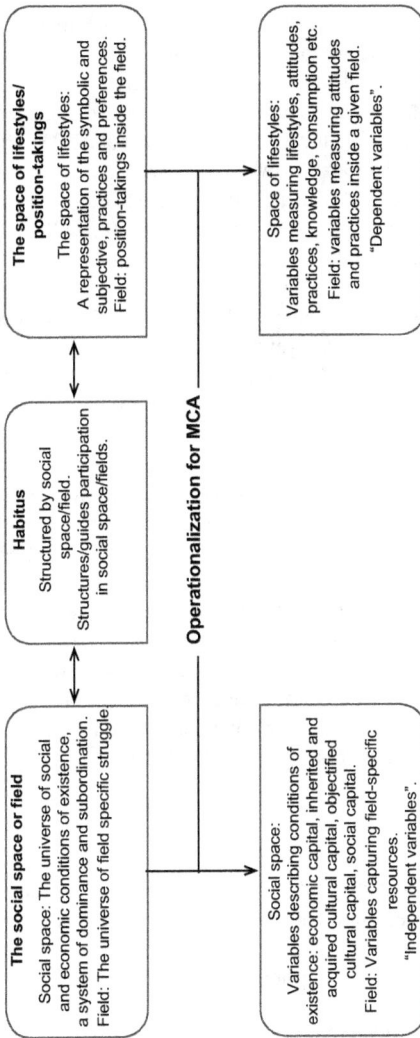

The social space or field

Social space: The universe of social and economic conditions of existence, a system of dominance and subordination.
Field: The universe of field specific struggle.

Habitus

Structured by social space/field.
Structures/guides participation in social space/fields.

The space of lifestyles/ position-takings

The space of lifestyles:
A representation of the symbolic and subjective, practices and preferences.
Field: position-takings inside the field.

Operationalization for MCA

Social space:
Variables describing conditions of existence: economic capital, inherited and acquired cultural capital, objectified cultural capital, social capital.
Field: Variables capturing field-specific resources.
"Independent variables".

Space of lifestyles:
Variables measuring lifestyles, attitudes, practices, knowledge, consumption etc.
Field: variables measuring attitudes and practices inside a given field.
"Dependent variables".

Figure 3.1 A re-worked version of Rosenlund's (2015) operational model of field theory

The social space/field model

The first method implies that a researcher measures people's access to different capital and based on this information creates a statistical representation of the social space. The coordinates of various lifestyles, such as media practices and preferences, can then be studied by including such traits as supplementary categories. This method applies when the researcher is concerned with society at large (or a "local" social space of a region or a city [Prieur et al., 2008]) and, in the follow-up step, how structures of domination/subordination are mirrored in people's lifestyles (Flemmen et al., 2018; Lindell, 2018). Alternatively, the method applies when we deal with distinct social fields, such as the journalistic field (Duval, 2005; Hovden, 2008), the cinematic field (Duval, 2016), or the field of television production (Lindell et al., 2020) and how positions in the field reflect in various position-takings (such as different occupational ideals and values within, for instance, the journalistic field). If the data needed to study a specific field is of historical character or in other ways difficult to attain using survey methods, the prosopographic method of data collection is a suitable alternative (see Chapter 5).

In regard to the social space, one of Bourdieu's main contributions was that in modern and differentiated societies, in which the state and the educational system have replaced the church in "sanctifying social divisions", there are two main forms of capital that "give access to positions of power": economic capital and cultural capital (Wacquant, 1996: x). By way of correspondence analysis, Bourdieu (1984) could show that the French social space in the 1960s and 1970s was structured, in the first instance, by overall volume of capital (high/low) and, in the second instance, by capital composition, separating social agents in terms of the extent to which their resources were primarily economic or cultural in character. By relying on the first method of the Bourdieusian approach to MCA (Figure 3.1), contemporary analyses have uncovered similar principles of social differentiation: capital volume and capital composition (e.g., Flemmen et al., 2018; Lindell, 2018, 2022; Rosenlund, 2019; Lindell et al., 2022).

The space of lifestyles/"reciprocal approach"

Rather than operationalizing cultural and economic capital (the social space approach) or field-specific resources (field analysis) and using these as active variables, the second method, the "reciprocal approach" (Lebart et al. in Rosenlund, 2015: 160), focuses primarily on the symbolic dimension of social life. Here, we begin by constructing a symbolic space (e.g., the space of media use [Hovden & Rosenlund, 2021; Purhonen et al., 2021; Sivertsen, 2023] or the space of cultural practices [Bennett et al., 2015; Hjellbrekke et al., 2015]). Herein the constellations of lifestyles and oppositions between, for instance, different types of media repertoires can be studied. Once this symbolic space is created, a range of demographic characteristics (such as gender, age, residential area, occupations, and access to various forms of capital) can be projected into the space as supplementary variables to study whether, and if so how, the symbolic universe is socially differentiated. In *Distinction* (Bourdieu, 1984), this method was used to study the tastes and lifestyles of different segments of the dominant social groups in French society. In a contemporary context, Atkinson's (2022) study of the US space of lifestyles reveals, in the first instance, that the universe of US lifestyles is structured by an opposition between "accessible" and "non-accessible" practices on the one hand, and between "high-brow" tastes and luxurious lifestyles on the other. In a second maneuver, social agents' capital endowments are mapped onto the space of lifestyles as supplementary variables. Atkinson shows that high volumes of capital correspond to the propensity to engage in "demanding" and "rare" activities (such as jazz and art museums). People's capital composition is mirrored in the taste for luxury goods such as cars, boats, and jewelry (economic capital) or "high-brow" activities such as attending classical concerts and galleries (cultural capital). From this, Atkinson concludes that the contemporary US space of lifestyles is "structured according to principles remarkably like those discovered in 1970s France by Bourdieu" (2022: 1076).

Homology

The two analytical strategies outlined above constitute a yin–yang model. The first method positions subjective orientations and position-takings in a class structure or in a specific field, while the second superimposes demographic variables on taste and lifestyle constellations. The two methods differ in respect to which variable group (variables capturing the "objective" positions versus variables that measure "subjective" orientations) is used as active and supplementary, respectively.

While the two methods complement one another, the realities and constraints of research in practice, in particular the limitations of the data that researchers have at their disposal, usually implies having to choose one of the methods. A survey rich in variables that measure media use allow the construction of a "space of media use" (Sivertsen, 2023) and treating demographic information (e.g., levels of education and incomes) as supplementary variables. Reversely, the researcher interested in the structure of class relations may have access to a survey rich in variables that measure different forms of capital but lacking the lifestyle variables necessary to construct the "symbolic" space. In this case, the social space strategy is preferred, and the partial information on people's lifestyles are used as supplementary variables (Lindell, 2022). In the best of worlds, however, we have access to rich survey data that allows the construction of both the social space and the space of lifestyles (Hovden & Rosenlund, 2021). This is a key to assessing one of Bourdieu's main contributions to cultural sociology: the homology thesis. This idea underpins the model illustrated in Figure 3.1, which stresses the intricate connection between the objective and the subjective character of social reality. The homology thesis posits that both the social space and the space of lifestyles are structured by the same principles:

> Bourdieu's theory /.../ asserts a connection between these two social universes. More precisely, his homology thesis claims that the principles of differentiation, volume and composition of capital, structure both spaces. In order to examine this relationship, we need knowledge about the properties of one space and project this information into the other space. We want to compare how the principle dimensions of one space, relate to the principle dimensions of the other.
>
> (Rosenlund, 2019: 10–11)

The question is, in other words, if both volume of capital and people's capital endowments reflect in lifestyles (e.g., see Rosenlund, 2015, 2019). In the Bourdieusian model (Figure 3.1), habitus serves as an "intermediate concept" (Bourdieu in Rosenlund, 2019: 3). Rather than a concept to be operationalized, habitus constitutes the theoretical explanation for why people's choices and values tend to correspond to their social position.

> These two universes are linked by the habitus. This mental structure is formed and moulded by agents' positions in social space and the experiences gained on their social trajectory into these positions. Their external social reality becomes incorporated and forms their inner, personal reality. However, the habitus is also structuring. It contains generative and creative instruments that agents use when taking stock of the social realities they encounter. A certain position in social space disposes the habitus to adopt certain categories of perception and classification, certain stances on political and ethical values, certain practices, inclinations, etc. Another position forms another habitus.
>
> (Rosenlund, 2019: 2–3, italics in original)

Beginnings: constructing the social space

To illustrate the Bourdieusian approach to MCA, we now turn to the analysis of the contemporary Swedish social space. This example follows the first method outlined in the previous section. In constructing the social space, a researcher usually relies on three to five indicators of economic capital (such as income, assets, land, and property) and a similar number of indicators of cultural capital (such as educational level, parents' education or occupations, educational subject area, and the "cultural" character of a person's childhood home) (Rosenlund, 2015). Sometimes, variables on respondents' positions in the labor market (e.g., occupational group or public or private employment) and social capital (e.g., the relative affluence of a person's social network, or board memberships) are also used as active variables (Rosenlund, 2015).

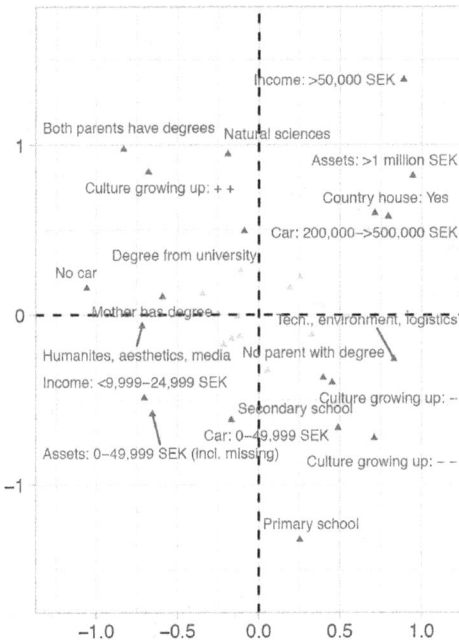

Figure 3.2 A model of the Swedish social space in 2020. Cloud of categories

Note: The "+" and "–" indicate the extent to which respondents agree/disagree with the statement that their childhood homes were rich cultural milieus

Figure 3.2 presents a statistical representation of the Swedish social space, showing the cloud of categories. It is based on an MCA of an online questionnaire answered by more than 2,000 Swedes above the age of 18 in 2020. The active variables used to measure respondents' cultural capital (in institutionalized, embodied, and objectified forms) were (1) parents' education, (2) access to cultural goods in the childhood home, (3) educational level, and (4) type of education. To capture economic capital, respondents were asked about their (1) monthly income, (2) second homes (summer house), (3) assets, and (4) the estimated value of their car(s) (see Table 3.1). In MCA, it is important that the active variables are re-coded so that they have roughly the same number of categories/values (Rosenlund, 2015). A variable with ten or more categories in an MCA where other variables hold only three categories could artificially skew the model. Likewise, variable categories catching less than 5 percent of the observations can also skew the model, and as such it is recommended to re-code the data in such a way that all categories accommodate more than five percent of the observations (Hjellbrekke, 2019).

A reader familiar with the MCA maps in *Distinction* (e.g., Bourdieu, 1984: 128–129) will recognize the structure of the Swedish social space represented

Table 3.1 Active re-coded variables for constructing the social space (Figure 3.2)

Active variable	Categories	N	%
Parents' education	No parent with degree	1148	59.1
	Mother has university degree	237	12.2
	Father has university degree	222	11.4
	Both parents have university degrees	334	17.2
Level of education	Primary school	245	12.2
	Secondary school	357	17.8
	Post-secondary school	518	25.9
	University degree	883	44.1
Home rich on culture when growing up	I completely agree (++)	438	21.9
	I agree somewhat (+)	755	37.7
	I disagree somewhat (−)	620	31.0
	I completely disagree (−−)	190	9.5
Education type	Social sciences, pedagogy, law	845	43.7
	Humanities, aesthetics, media	197	10.2
	Medicine, service	235	12.2
	Technology, environment, construction, logistics	439	22.7
	Natural sciences	218	11.3
Monthly income	<9,999–24,999 SEK/month	564	30.5
	25,000–34,999 SEK/month	536	29.0
	35,000–49,999 SEK/month	537	29.1
	>50,000 SEK/month	210	11.4
Assets/savings	0–49,999 SEK (including "don't know", refusal)	546	27.3
	50,000–249,999 SEK	582	29.1
	250,000–999,999 SEK	588	29.4
	>1 million SEK	287	14.3
Value of car(s)	Does not own car	500	25.0
	0–49,999 SEK	384	19.2
	50,000–199,999 SEK	710	35.4
	200,000–500,000 SEK	409	20.4
Country house	Does not own country house	1632	81.5
	Owns country house	371	18.5

in Figure 3.2. The figure displays the twenty variable categories that contribute most to the two axes/dimensions. Much like the results found in Bourdieu's analyses and those of others who have applied his research designs (Flemmen et al., 2018; Rosenlund, 2019), the two main axes capture capital composition and volume of capital. The first dimension describes discrepancies in social agents' structure of capital. This dimension explains 47 percent of the inertia and taps into the oppositions between different capital endowments. To the right in Figure 3.2 we find categories capturing economic affluence, whereas people whose capital portfolios are dominated by cultural capital are located on the left-hand side. The second dimension (42 percent of the inertia) captures an opposition between low (bottom of the figure) and high (top of the figure) volumes of different capitals.[1] Although the structure of the space clearly resembles Bourdieu's outline, this should not be viewed as an argument that contemporary Swedish society is exactly like French society in the 1970s (see Broady [1998] for a deeper discussion). Rather, the figure suggests the validity in the overarching, two-folded, logic of social differentiation in modern societies.

The distribution of the categories resembles the "chiastic" tendencies described by Bourdieu and others (Lebaron & Le Roux, 2018: 509). The volumes of cultural capital and economic capital follow a crisscross structure in the space: the lowest amounts of cultural capital are located in the bottom-right and the highest in the top-left quadrant, whereas the lowest volumes of economic capital are found in the bottom-left and the highest salaries and other material assets are found in the top-right. Categories in close proximity to one another "catch" the same individuals (Hjellbrekke, 2019). This means, for instance, that people who grew up with well-educated parents tend to be well-educated today, and that their childhood homes were filled with literature, art, music, and other cultural expressions. Likewise, people with high salaries also have significant assets and savings and are also more likely to own a second home and expensive cars. In the analysis of the social space, we move away from the study of "classes on paper" (Bourdieu, 1985), as the focus is on social agents sharing similar social positions, and by that token they constitute social groups, or classes. In this vein, we can speak of the people in the top-left quadrant as the cultural middle- and upper-class, and the people in the top-right as the economic middle- and upper-class. The "working class" (which designates an occupational category or a position in the mode of production) can be studied insofar as it is a social group characterized by relatively low volumes of capital, particularly cultural capital (bottom-right quadrant). Alternatively, variables on respondents' occupations are used either as supplementary or as active variables.

With Figure 3.3 we turn to the cloud of individuals. Should the cloud of individuals not display the fairly balanced and round shape we observe in Figure 3.3, the researcher can consider revisiting data for re-coding or analyzing more than two axes (see Hjellbrekke, 2019). Individuals located in close proximity to each other tend to share similar social positions (volumes and

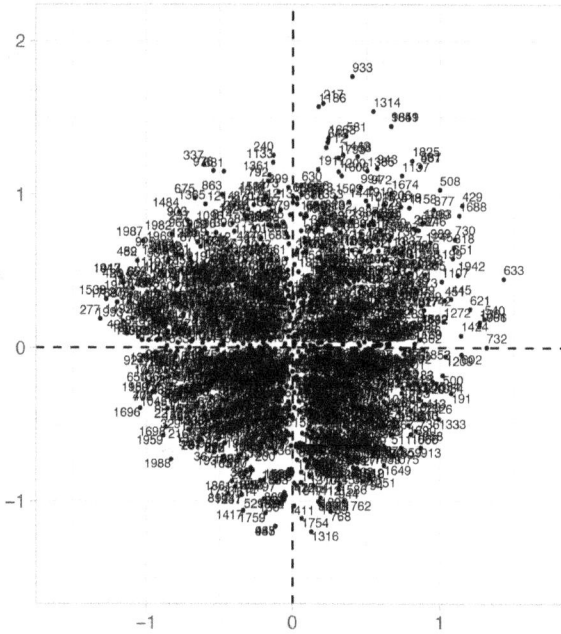

Figure 3.3 Cloud of individuals (Swedish social space 2020)

compositions of capital). This is further illustrated in using confidence ellipses to highlight the positions of the categories pertaining to the active variables. In Figure 3.4, we trace the distribution of the variable capturing parents' education and observe (in line with the chiastic structure of the space) that levels increase as we move toward the top-left quadrant in the space. Reversely, in Figure 3.5, we follow the variable "assets" and observe that respondents' wealth increases as we move toward the top-right quadrant.

This empirical example has illustrated one of the Bourdieusian models outlined in the previous section. Contrary to the "reciprocal" model where indicators of lifestyles are used as active variables to construct the space, we have here focused on the "objective" domain and the distribution of social resources in the population. The next step in the social space approach is, of course, to project a number of lifestyle variables, such as media use, into the social space, and study the extent to which these correspond to social positions. This implies that we leave the strictly sociological inquiry on the structure of the social space and move into the research questions relevant to media and communication studies. By projecting a range of media practices into the social space, as supplementary variables, we are allowed to study the extent to which people's media use follows social hierarchies. This will be the focus of Chapter 4. It

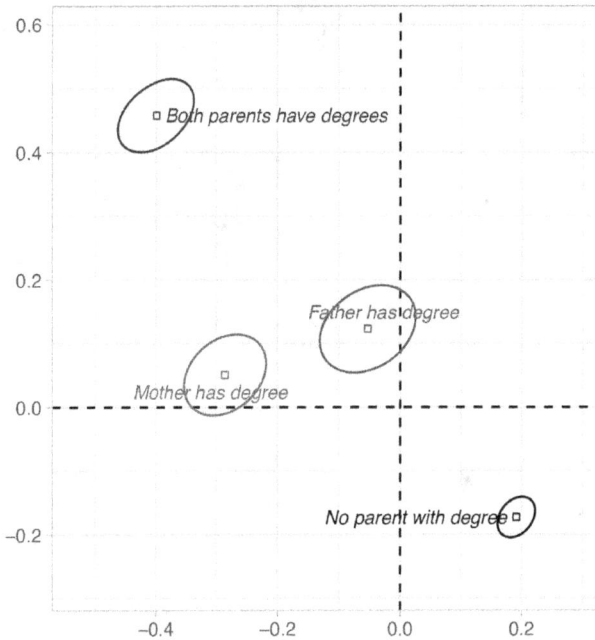

Figure 3.4 Confidence ellipses: parents' education

should be repeated that the strategy used in the example of the social space applies to the study of distinct social fields, although in such analyses the main focus is put on the distribution of field-specific capital among the "players" in a given field (e.g., Hovden, 2008; Duval, 2016; Lindell et al., 2020). Chapter 5 focuses on the study of the fields of media and cultural production.

Qualitative Bourdieu

In the 1950s, Bourdieu performed ethnographic fieldwork among the Kabyle in Algeria; in the 1960s and onwards, he turned to the study of the French social space, lifestyles, and elite fields. His career is marked by shifts in the object of study (e.g., from traditional to modern societies), theoretical development, and changing methodological propensities that can be summed up in the tendency to gradually favor quantitative methods (Sallaz, 2018). If his ethnographic studies of the Kabyle primarily focused on the habitus (and how it failed to attune itself to life in modern, urban capitalism), the later works on the school system and social differentiation in modern France shifted the theoretical balance in favor of the notions of capital, fields, and social space. Qualitative methods permeated Bourdieu's early work, appeared next to

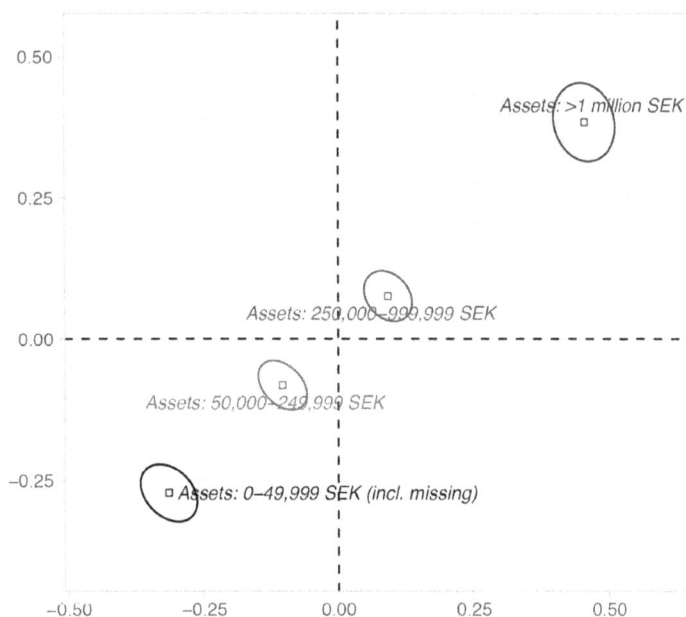

Figure 3.5 Confidence ellipses: assets

correspondence maps in *Distinction*, and lingered on in later works such as *The Weight of the World* (Bourdieu et al., 1999). *The Rules of Art* was based on the qualitative-sociological reading of not only Flaubert's novel *Sentimental Education* but also mail correspondences between key agents in the 19th-century French literary field. Much of his later research, however, demanded quantitative methods that would be able to "document the existence of social facts such as social fields" (Sallaz, 2018: 491) and study the systematic overlaps, or homologies, between social groups and the universe of lifestyles.

As noted in the introductory chapter, Bourdieu has many faces, and ethnographers and qualitative researchers oftentimes find in Bourdieu a "kindred spirit" (Sallaz, 2018: 481). But to scrutinize the social space and fields, we are required to rely on the relational and topological thinking of correspondence analysis. Bourdieu thus holds that the ethnographic method produces only partial knowledge. As with other strands in the "subjectivist" approach to the social world, ethnography fails to account for the broader structures of the social world. Put differently, the concepts of field and social space are "of an ontological status that essentially renders them invisible to ethnographic documentation" (Sallaz, 2018: 491).

These critiques of the ethnographic method notwithstanding, a Bourdieusian ethnography is, according to Sallaz (2018), still possible if fieldwork is contextualized in extra-local contexts (social space, field) and if it is systematic and reflexive in regard to the (scholastic) position of the researcher entering the empirical field. This is illustrated not least in the works of Bourdieu's disciple Loïc Wacquant (Wacquant & Vandebroeck, 2023). Since MCA is still only practiced among a small but growing group of media scholars, Bourdieu-inspired media and communication research tends to be qualitative in nature. The relatively large body of qualitative Bourdieusian media and communication scholarship testifies to the fact that field theory, at least parts of it, can be fruitfully put to use in qualitative media and communication studies. In audience research, Danielsson's (2014) work on the digital media practices of young men, Banjac's (2022) study of South African news audiences, and Hartley's (2018) interviews with young Danes all reveal clear links between social positions and media practices. In journalism studies, Schultz's (2007) ethnography of the newsroom and the journalistic "gut-feel" and Chew and Tandoc's (2024) interview study on the (journalistic) habitus of people in media startups stress the routinized character of news production, but also the potential mismatches (the so-called hysteresis effect) between a journalistic habitus and the rapidly changing journalistic field. Galli's (2012) ethnography of the Swedish field of brands constitutes an excellent in-depth account of the norms and hierarchies inside the world of marketing and PR.

While qualitative methods may not allow researchers to fully get a grasp of the abstract entities of social space and field, it is nonetheless still possible, albeit challenging, to rely on Bourdieu in qualitative research designs. Working with field theory qualitative researchers need to be aware that their methods produce partial knowledge and should thus consider taking measures to supplement their interest in the "minutiae of daily practices" (Bourdieu & Wacquant, 1992: 113) with methods that can contextualize practices in the "objective" structures that constitute the conditions within which practice unfolds. Qualitative methods can, nonetheless, supplement studies that rely on MCA in productive ways.

MCA and Bourdieusian analysis put high demands on data. In constructing the social space, a number of indicators are needed for both economic and cultural capital. To operationalize the field-specific resources in a given field, we need a basic idea of what those resources consist of. And to properly account for the structures of the space of lifestyles or the space of media use, a range of variables are required. MCA, furthermore, "provides only a 'summary' of the table submitted to it" (Duval, 2018: 517), and as such it provides "imperfect representations of fields" (Duval, 2018: 522). The task of the researcher is to make these representations as good as they can possibly get. If we remain loyal to the open-ended ambitions in the Bourdieusian framework, the task is to "identify the forms of specific capital that operate" in a given field and include these in the MCA (Bourdieu & Wacquant, 1992: 108). But how does one know which variables to include in an MCA? In other words, how does one know, prior to empirical investigation, which capitals operate in the field? In response to such questions, Duval (2018: 516) holds that MCA demands "a fairly advanced intuition of the principles structuring the space". It is safe to assume that many would be unsatisfied with this answer. This is where qualitative methods can fruitfully supplement statistical analysis and replace "intuition" with ethnographic understanding. Researchers would be well-off starting by putting "their nose to the ground" (Bourdieu & Wacquant, 1992: 113) with ethnographic observations, and conduct interviews in the given field in order to understand its main principles, hierarchies, and what properties function as capital. Indeed, interviews and observations preceded the construction of the surveys used for *Distinction* (de Saint Martin, 2015) as well as recent studies of the space of lifestyles (e.g., Bennett et al., 2015). Focus group interviews, for example the Q-method of sorting and ranking various media genres or outlets (Schrøder, 2016), can fruitfully be used to uncover the main contours of contemporary media repertoires. The findings can guide the process of operationalization for the purpose of constructing the space of media use with MCA. In this way, qualitative insights can guide the construction of the survey that is to be put in the field.

MCA excels in representing complex relations of domination and subordination, and in understanding the extent to which social groups reproduce their positions in how they move about in the social world (attitudes, dispositions, tastes, lifestyles). MCA cannot, however, get a grip on how such systemic differences are enacted in practice. This is where qualitative work on symbolic boundary drawing enters the picture. As Jarness (2018: 5) writes, Michelle Lamont has questioned the Bourdieusian assumption that the observed statistical correspondences between social positions and lifestyles would "lead directly to hierarchisation and group-formation". Using qualitative interviews, Lamont (1992) focused on the "repertoires of evaluation" used by social groups in order to set themselves apart from others. Similar approaches have been used to unearth how social groups discursively construct "an other" on the basis of the perceived lifestyles of people in different class positions (Jarness & Flemmen, 2019; Lindell, 2020; Lindell & Kas, 2024). In practice, this means interviewing individuals in different social positions, defined by their access to various forms of capital, and probe the ways in which they discursively construct boundaries between themselves and people occupying different positions in the social space. Such boundaries manifest, for instance, when people in the culturally rich middle class describe the working class as lazy, sedentary, and not properly updated on the news, or when people lacking cultural capital refer to those rich in cultural capital as "snobs" (Lindell, 2020). Needless to say, these studies draw upon careful coding of interview transcripts, and for these purposes discourse analysis and qualitative coding of interview transcripts should lie close at hand.

Interview studies attempting to reveal symbolic boundary drawing between social groups go to great lengths to ensure that the "objective" dimension pertaining to social life is accounted for in that interviewees are sampled on the basis of their access to economic and cultural capital. Ideally, however, qualitative interviews are combined with MCA. For instance, Jarness (2018) starts in an MCA of the Norwegian social space, and then proceeds to interview social agents in different social positions. Interviewees were provided with the same questionnaire as the respondents studied in the MCA, and as such it was possible to "project" interviewees onto the MCA maps and uncover their positions in the social space. This mixed-methods approach to the social space retains the topological focus on people's objective conditions of existence, while at the same time allowing the researcher to study position-takings and symbolic boundary drawing in a qualitative manner.

Conclusion

This chapter has covered the epistemological principles of field theory and illustrated how they are translated into empirical work with MCA. Field theory presents a conceptual toolkit used in constructing the object of study, but it is at the same time open-ended and geared toward letting theory develop in tandem with empirical research. The chapter has discussed two main operational Bourdieusian models for empirical research: the social space/field approach and the "reciprocal" or "symbolic" approach. The craft of Bourdieusian research was illustrated by constructing and analyzing the main oppositions in the Swedish social space. The chapter concluded with a discussion on Bourdieu's approach to qualitative methods and presented examples on how ethnography, qualitative interviews, and discourse analysis can supplement empirical work within the MCA tradition. In the next chapters we will delve deeper into research questions pertaining to media and communication studies. Chapter 4 focuses on a range of media practices in relation to the social space. In Chapter 5, we move away from the study of social space to instead cover the distinct social fields of media and cultural production. This chapter has not covered social network analysis and the study of social relations in digital milieus. Such analyses remain outside of the mainstream methodology of Bourdieusian sociology and require theoretical and methodological re-calibration. This will be the focus of Chapter 6.

Box 3.2   Steps in Bourdieusian research

The following list presents the main steps undertaken in Bourdieusian media studies using survey data. A reader looking for detailed statistical introductions to MCA is referred to Le Roux and Rouanet (2010) and Hjellbrekke (2019).

1 **Construct the research question.** Is the project concerned with relations of domination and subordination in society at large, a particular "symbolic space" (such as the space of media use), or a distinct social field (such as the journalistic field)?

2 **Decide on which Bourdieusian model to use.** Will the focus be on the structure of a field, the social space, or on the dimensions in a particular lifestyle domain? Will the data allow both approaches?

3 **Ethnographic phase.** Put the "nose to the ground" and reach an initial understanding of the social space/field in question, making it possible to "identify the forms of specific capital that operate" (Bourdieu & Wacquant, 1992: 108) or the main lifestyle discrepancies (Bennett et al., 2015) in the given setting.

4 **Design the survey.** For the social space/field approach, first make sure that the survey includes measurements of all relevant capitals, and in a second instance operationalize media practices. For the "reciprocal approach", make sure to capture all relevant lifestyle manifestations (a study on news consumption, for instance, will need to capture all relevant news outlets and position-takings that agents might have in regard to journalism) and in a second instance operationalize demographics/capitals.

5 **Overview the data.** Get acquainted with the data and its tendencies through basic statistical analyses (frequency tables, contingency tables, correlations, etc.).

6 **Cleaning and re-coding phase.** Clean your data and remove "junk" categories and missing values. Re-code the data so that variable values capture >5 percent of the observations.

7 **Initial MCA runs.** Decide on which active variables to use in the construction of the space. Study the contributions to the axes/dimensions and the shape of the cloud of individuals (see, e.g., Hjellbrekke, 2019). It might be necessary to return to phase 6 and re-code the data.

8 **Interpret axes/dimensions.** Study as many dimensions as needed in order to be able to account for 80 percent of the inertia (one of several rules of thumb for the selection of which axes to focus on). Note the contribution of variables and categories to the axes/ dimensions. Qualitatively interpret the dimensions and their meaning (– what oppositions are captured?).

9 **Project supplementary variables.** In the social space/field approach: project lifestyles, position-takings, practices, and preferences into the space and study their coordinates. In the "reciprocal approach": identify the positions' demographics and access to various capitals in the space. Distances on paper indicate social distances (Bourdieu, 1989). Deviations above .5 from the center of the space are considered notable, although weaker associations can be sociologically interesting.

10 **(Re-)theorize.** Do findings "refute" or "generalize" (Bourdieu, 1991: 255)?

Note

1 Due to limited space, there is no room to display all tables one would prefer to show for readers to be able to fully estimate the construction of the social space and its interpretation. In regard to the contribution of the active variables to the two axes in Figure 3.2 (the Swedish social space), the Eta^2 values for dimension 1 (capital composition) were: "Value of car" = .444, "Parents' level of education" = .259, "Assets" .258, "Income" = .254, "Type of education" = .232, "Culture growing up" = .219, "Summer house" = .118, and "Level of education" = .067. For dimension 2 (capital volume), the Eta^2 values were: "Level of education" = .350, "Income" = . 341, "Parents' level of education" = .256, "Culture growing up" = .255, "Assets" = . 195, "Value of car" = .153, "Type of education" = .125, and "Summer house" = .083. For axis 1 (capital composition), the ten active categories that contribute most are (in hierarchical order): "no car", "tech., logistics etc.", "<9,999–24,499 SEK/ month", "Assets: >1 mil", "Car: 200,000–>500,000", "Both parents have degrees", "Culture growing up: ++", "Country house: Yes", ">50,000 SEK/month" and "No parent with degree". For axis 2 (capital volume), the ten active categories that contribute most are (in hierarchical order): ">50,000 SEK/month", "Both parents have degrees", "Culture growing up: ++", "Primary school", "Degree from university", "Assets: >1 mil", "Natural sciences", "No parent with degree", "Secondary school", "Assets: 0–49,999 SEK".

References

Atkinson, W. (2016). Class and cuisine in contemporary Britain reheated: A reply to Flemmen and Hjellbrekke. *The Sociological Review, 64*(1), 194–201.

Atkinson, W. (2022). The US Space of lifestyles and its homologies. *Sociological Perspectives, 65*(6), 1060–1080.

Banjac, S. (2022). An intersectional approach to exploring audience expectations of journalism. *Digital Journalism, 10*(1), 128–147.

Bennett, T., Bustamante, M., & Frow, J. (2015). The Australian space of lifestyles in comparative perspective. In P. Coulangeon & J. Duval (Eds.), *The Routledge companion to Bourdieu's Distinction* (pp. 255–282). London, New York: Routledge.

Benson, R. (1999). Field theory in comparative context: A new paradigm for media studies. *Theory and Society, 28*(3), 463–498.

Blumer, H. (1956). Sociological analysis and the "variable". *American Sociological Review, 21*(6), 683–690.

Bourdieu, P. (1984). *Distinction: A social critique of the judgement of taste.* New York: Routledge.

Bourdieu, P. (1985). The social space and the genesis of groups. *Social Science Information, 24*(2), 195–220.

Bourdieu, P. (1986). The forms of capital. In J. G. Richardson (Ed.), *Handbook of theory and research for the sociology of education* (pp. 241–258). New York, Greenwood: Greenwood Press.

Bourdieu, P. (1989). Social space and symbolic power. *Sociological Theory, 7*(1), 14–25.

Bourdieu, P. (1990). *The logic of practice.* Stanford, CA: Stanford University Press.

Bourdieu, P. (1991). Meanwhile, I have come to know all the diseases of sociological understanding. In P. Bourdieu, J.-C. Chamboredon, & J.-C. Passeron (Eds.), *The craft of sociology: Epistemological preliminaries* (pp. 247–259). Berlin, New York: Walter de Gruyter.

Bourdieu, P. (2000a). *Konstens regler: Det litterära fältets uppkomst och struktur* [The rules of art: Genesis and structure of the literary field]. Stockholm: Brutus Östlings Bokförlag.

Bourdieu, P. (2000b). *Pascalian meditations*. Cambridge: Polity.

Bourdieu, P. (2013). Symbolic capital and social classes. *Journal of Classical Sociology, 13*(2), 292–302.

Bourdieu, P., & Passeron, J.-C. (1990). *Reproduction in education, society and culture*. Los Angeles: Sage.

Bourdieu, P., & Wacquant, L. (1992). *An invitation to reflexive sociology*. Cambridge: Polity.

Bourdieu, P., Accardo, A., Balazs, G., Beaud, S. et al. (1999). *The weight of the world: Social suffering in contemporary society*. Stanford, CA: Stanford University Press.

Broady, D. (1998). *Kapitalbegreppet som utbildningssociologiskt verktyg* [The concept of capital as a tool in educational sociology]. ILU: Skeptron Occasional Papers no. 15. Uppsala University.

Broady, D. (2002). French prosopography: Definition and suggested readings. *Poetics, 30*(5–6), 381–385.

Chew, M., & Tandoc, E. C., Jr. (2024). Media startups are behaving more like tech startups—iterative, multi-skilled and journalists that "hustle". *Digital Journalism, 12*(2), 191–211.

Coulangeon, P., Demoli, Y., & Petev, I. D. (2015). Cultural distinction and material consumption: The case of cars in contemporary France. In P. Coulangeon & J. Duval (Eds.), *The Routledge companion to Bourdieu's Distinction* (pp. 119–131). London, New York: Routledge.

Danielsson, M. (2014). *Digitala distinktioner: Klass och kontinuitet i unga mäns vardagliga mediepraktiker*. [Doctoral dissertation, School of Education and Communication, Jönköping University].

de Saint Martin, M. (2015). From "Anatomie du gout" to La Distinction: Attempting to construct the social space: Some markers for the history of research. In P. Coulangeon & J. Duval (Eds.), *The Routledge companion to Bourdieu's Distinction* (pp. 15–28). London, New York: Routledge.

Duval, J. (2005). Economic journalism in France. In R. Benson & E. Neveu (Eds.), *Bourdieu and the journalistic field* (pp. 135–155). Cambridge: Polity.

Duval, J. (2016). *Le Cinéma au XXe siècle. Entre loi du marché et règles de l'art*. Paris: CNRS editions.

Duval, J. (2018). Correspondence analysis and Bourdieu's use of statistics: Using correspondence analysis within field theory. In T. Medvetz & J. J. Sallaz (Eds.), *The Oxford handbook of Pierre Bourdieu* (pp. 512–527). Oxford: Oxford University Press.

Emirbayer, M. (1997). Manifesto for a relational sociology. *American Journal of Sociology, 103*(2), 281–317.

Flemmen, M., & Hjellbrekke, J. (2016). Response: Not so fast: A comment on Atkinson and Deeming's "Class and cuisine in contemporary Britain: The social space, the space of food and their homology". *The Sociological Review, 64*(1), 184–193.

Flemmen, M., Jarness, V., & Rosenlund, L. (2018). Social space and cultural class divisions: The forms of capital and contemporary lifestyle differentiation. *The British Journal of Sociology, 69*(1), 124–153.

Galli, R. (2012). *Varumärkenas fält: produktion av erkännande i Stockholms reklam-värld* [The field of brands: The production of recognition in Stockholm's marketing world]. [Doctoral dissertation, Acta Universitatis Stockholmiensis].

Ginsburger, M. (2022). The more it changes the more it stays the same: The French social space of material consumption between 1985 and 2017. *The British Journal of Sociology, 73*(4), 706–753.

Greenacre, M., & Blasius, J. (Eds.). (2006). *Multiple correspondence analysis and related methods.* London: CRC Press.

Grossberg, L. (1995). Cultural studies vs. political economy: Is anybody else bored with this debate? *Critical Studies in Mass Communication, 12*(1), 72–81.

Habermas, J. (1989). *The structural transformation of the public sphere: An inquiry into a category of bourgeois society.* Cambridge, MA: MIT Press.

Hartley, J. M. (2018). "It's something posh people do": Digital distinction in young people's cross-media news engagement. *Media and Communication, 6*(2), 46–55.

Hjellbrekke, J. (2019). *Multiple correspondence analysis for the social sciences.* London: Routledge.

Hjellbrekke, J., Jarness, V., & Korsnes, O. (2015). Cultural distinctions in an "egalitarian" society. In P. Coulangeon & J. Duval (Eds.), *The Routledge companion to Bourdieu's Distinction* (pp. 187–206). London, New York: Routledge.

Hovden, J. F. (2008). *Profane and sacred. A Study of the Norwegian journalistic field.* Bergen: University of Bergen.

Hovden, J. F., & Rosenlund, L. (2021). Class and everyday media use: A case study from Norway. *Nordicom Review, 42*(s3), 129–149.

Jarness, V. (2018). Viewpoints and points of view: Situating symbolic boundary drawing in social space. *European Societies, 20*(3), 503–524.

Jarness, V., & Flemmen, M. P. (2019). A struggle on two fronts: Boundary drawing in the lower region of the social space and the symbolic market for "down-to-earthness". *The British Journal of Sociology, 70*(1), 166–189.

Lamont, M. (1992). *Money, morals, and manners: The culture of the French and the American upper-middle class.* Chicago: University of Chicago Press.

Latour, B. (2005). *Reassembling the social: An introduction to actor-network-theory.* Oxford: Oxford University Press.

Le Roux, B., & Rouanet, H. (2010). *Multiple correspondence analysis.* London: SAGE.

Lebaron, F., & Le Roux, B. (2018). Bourdieu and geometric data analysis. In T. Medvetz & J. J. Sallaz (Eds.), *The Oxford handbook of Pierre Bourdieu* (pp. 503–511). Oxford: Oxford University Press.

Lindell, J. (2018). *Distinction* recapped: Digital news repertoires in the class structure. *New Media & Society, 20*(8), 3029–3049.

Lindell, J. (2020). Battle of the classes: News consumption inequalities and symbolic boundary work. *Critical Studies in Media Communication, 37*(5), 480–496.

Lindell, J. (2022). Symbolic violence and the social space: Self-imposing the mark of disgrace? *Cultural Sociology, 16*(3), 379–401.

Lindell, J., & Hovden, J. F. (2018). Distinctions in the media welfare state: Audience fragmentation in post-egalitarian Sweden. *Media, Culture & Society, 40*(5), 639–655.

Lindell, J., Jakobsson, P., & Stiernstedt, F. (2020). The field of television production: Genesis, structure and position-takings. *Poetics, 80*, 101432.

Lindell, J., Jansson, A., & Fast, K. (2022). I'm here! Conspicuous geomedia practices and the reproduction of social positions on social media. *Information, Communication & Society, 25*(14), 2063–2082.

Lindell, J., & Kas, A. D. (2024). Media practice and class-making: The anticipation of stigma and the cultural middle-class habitus. *Media, Culture & Society, 46*(1), 21–37.

Marzec, P. M. (2019). *Distinction in Poland. Testing elements of the Bourdieusian theory of class.* [Doctoral Dissertation, University of Bristol].

Neveu, E. (2005). Bourdieu, the Frankfurt school, and cultural studies: On some misunderstandings. In R. Benson & E. Neveu (Eds.), *Bourdieu and the journalistic field* (pp. 195–213). Cambridge: Polity.

Peterson, R. A. (1992). Understanding audience segmentation: From elite and mass to omnivore and univore. *Poetics, 21,* 243–258.

Prieur, A., Rosenlund, L., & Skjott-Larsen, J. (2008). Cultural capital today: A case study from Denmark. *Poetics, 36*(1), 45–71.

Purhonen, S., Leguina, A., & Heikkilä, R. (2021). The space of media usage in Finland, 2007 and 2018: The impact of online activities on its structure and its association with sociopolitical divisions. *Nordicom Review, 42*(S3), 111–128.

Rosenlund, L. (2015). Working with Distinction: Scandinavian experiences. In P. Coulangeon & J. Duval (Eds.), *The Routledge companion to Bourdieu's Distinction* (pp. 157–186). London, New York: Routledge.

Rosenlund, L. (2019). The persistence of inequalities in an era of rapid social change. Comparisons in time of social spaces in Norway. *Poetics, 74,* 101323.

Sallaz, J. J. (2018). Is a Bourdieusian ethnograhy possible? In T. Medvetz & J. J. Sallaz (Eds.), *The Oxford handbook of Pierre Bourdieu* (pp. 481–502). Oxford: Oxford University Press.

Sapiro, G. (2002). The structure of the French literary field during the German occupation (1940–1944): A multiple correspondence analysis. *Poetics, 30*(5–6), 387–402.

Savage, M., & Silva, E. B. (2013). Field analysis in cultural sociology. *Cultural Sociology, 7*(2), 111–126.

Schröder, K. C. (2016). Q-method and news audience research. In T. Witschge, C. W. Anderson, D. Domingo, & A. Hermida (Eds.), *The Sage handbook of digital journalism* (pp. 528–545). London: SAGE Publications.

Schultz, I. (2007). The journalistic gut feeling: Journalistic doxa, news habitus and orthodox news values. *Journalism Practice, 1*(2), 190–207.

Sivertsen, M. F. (2023). Stratified public connections—beyond the taste for news? *Journalism Studies,* 1–21.

Toft, M. (2022). Quantifying class trajectories: Linking topological and temporal accounts. *Bulletin of Sociological Methodology/Bulletin de Méthodologie Sociologique, 154*(1), 105–132.

Wacquant, L. (1996). Foreword. In P. Bourdieu, *The state nobility* (pp. ix–xxii). Cambridge: Polity.

Wacquant, L. (2018). Four transversal principles for putting Bourdieu to work. In T. Medvetz & J. J. Sallaz (Eds.), *The Oxford handbook of Pierre Bourdieu* (pp. 643–653). Oxford: Oxford University Press.

Wacquant, L., & Vandebroeck, D. (2023). Carnal concepts in action: The diagonal sociology of Loïc Wacquant. *Thesis Eleven,* 07255136221149782.

4 The social space and media use

Introduction

This chapter focuses on the Bourdieusian study of media audiences and users through multiple correspondence analysis (MCA). In previous chapters and elsewhere (Lindell, forthcoming), I have argued that the common notions of users and audiences carry limiting epistemological implications. The main drawback is that the manifold practices pertaining to everyday life, and the objective conditions that shape the ways in which social agents maneuver in everyday life, remain unaccounted for (see also Madianou, 2009). Indeed, "users" and "audiences" seemingly do little else than use the media, and thus "the possession of a television transforms a shipyard worker and a rural merchant into a 'television viewer'" (Neveu, 2005: 198). In combatting such media-centric tendencies, the Bourdieusian approach posits people as social agents. At this stage, the reader is familiar with this category, and knows that the notion of social agent is deployed to stress that people occupy specific positions in the social space, set by access to various forms of capital (Bourdieu, 1984). The positions in a given social structure, social trajectories and movements through the educational system, and participation in various social fields imply that social agents apprehend the social world in specific ways. This is likely reflected in how people use and relate to various media.

The notion of media practice, understood via Couldry (2004: 117) as "the open set of practices relating to, or oriented around, media", is particularly useful in this context, as it opens up for a range of research questions and focal points. Media practice, in Couldry's use of the term, designates everything from watching television to (dis)trusting the news and browsing social media – it focuses on what people *do* and *think* in relation to media. A related concept in contemporary audience research is media repertoires, which defines the "specific combination of contacts with different media and kinds of content" (Hasebrink & Popp, 2006: 384). The notion captures the fact that in contemporary digital media landscapes, people's patterns of media use are "inherently cross-media" (Schrøder, 2011). In this chapter I use the notion of media practice to describe what people do and think in relation to media, and

DOI: 10.4324/9781003364245-4

media repertoires to designate the constellations of specific preferences and practices in regard to the cultural goods on offer in the current media landscape. At the general level, media practices and media repertoires should be conceptualized as part of broader lifestyles and thus linked to other tastes and practices.

In Bourdieusian sociology, various media practices (such as news consumption or television viewing) are often included in the analysis of broad lifestyle patterns, particularly as part of the active variables used to study the space of lifestyles (see, e.g., the numerous analyses of this kind in Coulangeon & Duval, 2015). Being occupied by lifestyles in the broad sense, MCA-oriented sociologists oftentimes make little effort to analyze the peculiarities of media practices and their particular social functions. While recent research suggests this is changing (Cvetičanin et al., 2024) media researchers are well-positioned to contribute to the field of cultural sociology and Bourdieusian scholarship in two distinct ways. First, media scholars make explicit the fact that contemporary lifestyles are thoroughly mediatized, which suggests that culture consumption (or "consumer culture" or "lifestyles") today is virtually inseparable from "media culture" (Jansson, 2002). That is to say that a significant share of what we do in everyday life is (increasingly) reliant on media of various kinds. It is, in other words, increasingly difficult to think of lifestyles not affected by mediatization and how the affordances of various media alter culture consumption (e.g., Hjarvard, 2013). A key example here is how social media have made culture consumption and lifestyles more conspicuous (in terms of broadcasting not only lifestyles, achievements but also whereabouts) (Lindell et al., 2022). Secondly, media scholars bring a sensitivity toward discrepancies between various media practices: there are, for instance, qualitative differences between reading (different types of) current affairs and listening to (various genres of) music. For instance, the study of hours spent watching television or reading the news is not particularly telling in the detailed analysis of social differentiation in media practice. Particular genres and modes of consumption need to be unpacked to add a sensitivity in constructing the object of study and designing Bourdieusian studies of media practices. However, while certain media practices are ontologically special, for example, in that they allow people to form "public lifestyles" (Hovden, 2023) through which they connect to the public sphere, they should still be analyzed in regard to the broader space of lifestyles (Bengtsson, 2015; Hovden & Moe, 2017; Lindell, 2018; Sivertsen, 2023).

The chapter begins by discussing Bourdieu's approach to the relationship between lifestyles and social positions. It then turns to empirical explorations of three domains of media practices in the social space. In empirical research, the Bourdieusian approach accommodates two distinct methods (see Chapter 3). In studying media practices, we can focus on the social space as such and rely on a statistical representation of the structure of class relations, and in a second instance study the distribution of various media practices therein. Alternatively, we focus on a particular domain of media practice (e.g., the practices and preferences connected to news and journalism, or the space of smartphone uses). In the latter "reciprocal" approach (Lebart et al. in Rosenlund, 2015: 160), MCA is used to tease out the main oppositions among variables measuring media practices/repertoires, and in the second step demographic information is projected as supplementary variables. While this chapter discusses both approaches, the empirical examples are drawn from the social space approach.

Bourdieu, lifestyles, and media practices

For Bourdieu (1984, 2013), the social world exists twice – in the objective distribution of capitals and in the symbolic representations that agents have of this world. These two realms are joined together by habitus. The habitus is the classificatory schemes of perception, valuation, and taste that promote lifestyles, including media practices. It is the product of the objective conditions under which agents were socialized, which includes but is not limited to parents' occupations and material and symbolic assets (such as cultural capital). Formed as it is in socialization processes and throughout trajectories in the educational system and other fields, the habitus is a durable system of classification – it is "a present past that tends to perpetuate itself into the future" (Bourdieu, 1990: 54). In regard to lifestyles this implies that "social agents have, *more often than one might expect*, dispositions (tastes, for example) that are more systematic than one might think" (Bourdieu, 2000: 64, italics in original). Among Bourdieu's writings it is in *Distinction* (1984) that the relationship between the social space and lifestyle is most clearly spelled out.

Box 4.1   A closer look at *Distinction*

Distinction was published in 1979 and has since been translated into 12 languages (including English in 1984) and remains Bourdieu's most cited work (Sapiro, 2015). The book innovated the study of social class and how inequalities are reflected in everyday life. Bourdieu studies French society in the 1960s and 1970s using ethnographic observations and interviews, newspaper clippings, photographs, and MCA.

Distinction argues that taste, as manifested in political opinions, media practices, home furnishings, sporting interests, music preferences, and other leisure pursuits, constitutes means through which social groups distinguish themselves from others and by extension "legitimize social differences" (Bourdieu, 1984: 7). Some social groups are better equipped, through their habitus, to navigate in the fine arts and other legitimized forms of culture. For others, this kind of culture is alien, "not for the likes of us" (1984: 471) or something to

---

be mimicked ("the cultural goodwill" of the petty bourgeoise). As such "every practice is bound to function as a *distinctive sign* and, when the difference is recognized, legitimate and approved, as a *sign of distinction*" (Bourdieu, 1991: 237: italics in original).

Those who have read *Distinction* might remember the perplexing maps of the relationships between different lifestyles and social positions. On pages 128–129, we are faced with a two-dimensional space of social positions, similar to the one explored in Chapter 3. At the top of the space, we find individuals endowed with high volumes of capital – they have both high salaries and high levels of education, and they tend to have grown up in relatively privileged social conditions. At the bottom are individuals relatively deprived of both economic and cultural capital. On one side of the space, we find individuals whose assets are primarily made up of cultural capital, and on the other side we find people who mainly have economic capital at their disposal. By also taking into account *what* people's social resources consist of, primarily either cultural or economic capital, Bourdieu presents what would become a key contribution to sociology: that social differentiation takes place not only "vertically" but also alongside a capital composition axis. The differences between "cultural" and "economic" factions in the social space are reflected in the struggles between different social fields – between cultural producers, intellectuals, and notions of "art for art's sake" on the one hand and political and economic powers in society on the other (Bourdieu, 1996).

Several correspondence analyses of survey data led to the conclusion that social differentiation revolved around the principles of capital volume and capital composition (de Saint Martin, 2015). *Distinction*, of course, was not only a contribution to the understanding of modern societies and their class structures. Projected onto Bourdieu's construction of the space of lifestyles are various lifestyles and tastes. The result of these analyses, and one of Bourdieu's main points, the homology thesis, is that taste and lifestyle hierarchies tend to follow social hierarchies. This means, for example, that the taste for the "legitimate" culture is rooted in a particular region in the social space, particularly among agents in possession of high volumes of cultural capital. In contrast, the working class, defined by its low levels of capital where the lack of cultural capital is particularly prominent, is more likely to *not* have an opinion on various cultural goods, or to dislike what the "cultural elite" likes. In Bourdieu's analyses, the inheritors of cultural capital – cultural producers, intellectuals, teachers, and public sector officials – spend their time on art exhibitions, chess, avantgarde culture, and *Le Monde*. The economic factions are drawn to golf, cocktail parties, the latest technological gadgets, and

Le Figaro. The corresponding groups at the lower end of the social space enjoy watching sports, rugby, playing/listening to the accordion (lack of cultural capital), cooking, and do-it-yourself practices (lacking economic capital) (1984: 128–129). Bourdieu concludes that there is a statistical overlap, or homology, between social space and the range of cultural goods and practices available in a society at a given time (the space of lifestyles). As noted in Chapter 3, the non-substantialist epistemology of Bourdieu's sociology implies that the correspondence between social positions and particular lifestyle manifestations is likely to assume different shapes in different contexts (i.e., they would change over both time and space).

With *Distinction,* Bourdieu shows that practices and preferences usually framed as individual peculiarities must be understood sociologically. Hobbies, Spotify lists, diets, film preferences and so on, which on the surface appear to stem from altogether individual traits and personal choice, must be understood as bound up in social regularities and linked to the structure of the social space. The objective conditions – upbringing, level of education, profession, and so on – give rise to a subjective moral and cultural compass, a habitus, that prompts us to orient ourselves in social life in a way that corresponds to our position in the social space. Affluence and prestige are reproduced in the internalization of a particular taste. Conversely, the resistance sometimes found in capital-poor segments of the population – the feeling that one does not understand opera and modern art or that politics is "not for me" – usually leads these social groups to cement their already subordinate position in society.

Part of the early reception of Bourdieu amongst media scholars reveals a skepticism toward the idea that the connections between lifestyles and social inequality could be transposed into the realm of media practices. Indeed, the notion of "mass media" stresses the capacity of the printed press, television, and radio to create "imagined communities" (Anderson, 1983) by virtue of their capacity to reach nation-wide audiences simultaneously. Bourdieu was, however, skeptical of notions of "mass media", "mass audiences", and "popular culture", which tend to presuppose "massive, passive, docile, credulous reception" (Bourdieu & Passeron in Neveu, 2005: 199) at odds with the idea that cultural goods are appropriated differently across social space.

Focusing on television in the 1990s, Garnham (1993: 188) suggested that "what we appear to see with television is a breaking down of the class-specific patterns of consumption that Bourdieu identifies elsewhere". In a similar vein, Couldry's notion of "media meta-capital" suggests that the mass media possess the potential to shape the habitus of agents across virtually all social fields

(2003: 668; see also Hjarvard, 2013). In their study of cultural practices in Great Britain, Bennett and colleagues found that film and television choices were "relatively weakly marked in class terms" (2009: 133). However, they note, like Bourdieu (1984), that television is a "negative asset" in that heavy television viewing tends to correspond to positions characterized by the lack of capital.

This narrative has changed in the digital media environment, as the mass media landscape has transitioned into one of "high choice" and the internet optimism of the 1990s has settled. Studies show that disparities in cultural participation and media use actually are greater online than offline (Kalogeropoulos & Nielsen, 2018; Mihelj et al., 2019). In his study on political communication in "post-broadcast democracy", Prior (2007) echoes the now-classic knowledge-gap hypothesis (Tichenor et al., 1970) and argues that the increasingly choice-oriented media landscape is likely to "exacerbate inequality" (Prior, 2007: 258), and Bolin posits that digital media users "consume objects and commodities that in the act of consumption produce difference" (2011: 86). Social agents transcend the universalizing force of the mass media and curate their own media repertoires from a vast array of services, channels, and devices. The ability to do so, however, "implies specific skills and knowledge – in short, cultural capital" (Mihelj et al., 2019: 1469). The current media landscape highlights the importance of habitus in the curation of media practices and repertoires, both in terms of the expanded market of cultural goods and in regard to the algorithmically geared feedback-loops provided by the platforms through which significant parts of contemporary culture consumption take place (Gaw, 2022; Lundahl, 2022).

It is in the context of the digital, "high-choice" media landscape that we have seen an increase in Bourdieu-inspired MCA studies of the relationship between the social space and various media practices, including news consumption, internet use, and film and TV preferences and so on (e.g., Hovden & Moe, 2017; Lindell, 2018; Hovden & Rosenlund, 2021; Leguina & Downey, 2021). These studies come together in stressing that disparities in media practices originate in access to various forms of capital. The differentiated distribution of media practices in the social space is explained by the fact that media practices "demand" a specific habitus and certain capitals. The symbolic mastery required to "properly" understand the avantgarde culture, independent films, improvised jazz, the stakes and positions in the culture debate in the quality newspapers suggest that social agents rich in cultural capital are more likely to form media repertoires corresponding to a "legitimate" taste. Likewise, purchasing the latest TV-set, sound system, and smartphone model, or the best seats at the theater, requires some degree of economic capital (e.g., Flemmen et al., 2018).

Digital distinctions in the hyper-connected welfare state

The present analyses of the social space and media practices take Sweden as a case study. In comparative research, Sweden is framed as a part of a

Northern media system (Brüggemann et al., 2014) or "media welfare state" (Syvertsen et al., 2014). This media system stands out internationally as it is characterized by generous subsidies and public financial support to the media (e.g., public service media and media subsidies for the private media market), high trust in the news (particularly in public service media), journalistic professionalism and autonomy, universal ambitions on access to media and communications, and deep digital penetration (Syvertsen et al., 2014). Recent developments are nonetheless presenting challenges to the institutions and normative principles underpinning this media system. Political polarization in media trust, the erosion of the political consensus around the role and function of public service media, and shifts in media subsidy policies (from ensuring diversity in the media market to upholding the market as such) suggest that the Swedish media system is moving in (neo)liberal directions (Jakobsson et al., 2021). Additionally, the globalization and digitalization of the media landscape, epitomized in streaming platforms such as Netflix and Spotify and social network sites, such as TikTok, imply a significant increase in the extent to which media users curate personal media repertoires. In this setting, it is worthwhile asking about the extent to which we can observe fragmentation on the "demand" side of the media landscape and ask about the disparities among media users (social agents).

In parallel to the structural transformations of the Swedish media system, the Social Democratic welfare state that developed between the 1940s and the 1970s has seen significant changes (Baeten et al., 2015). Economic inequality and social segregation have increased since the 1980s (Therborn, 2020). While higher education is publicly subsidized, there are clear trends of social reproduction in terms of young Swedes' (1) inclination to pursue studies at the tertiary level, (2) the selection of universities, and (3) the choice of study discipline. Children to well-educated professionals are significantly more likely to pursue higher education in the first place, and to enroll in prestigious universities such as the universities of Uppsala and Lund, The Stockholm School of Economics, and the Royal Institute of Technology, and to study high-status disciplines such as medicine, fine arts, and law (Börjesson, 2016). As already explored in the analysis of the Swedish social space (Chapter 3), we may conclude that the distribution of both economic and cultural capital is one characterized by inequality, heredity, and social reproduction.

Although both the media system and the political system move in directions that render Sweden less of an outlier in international comparisons, it seems as if this country, like other Scandinavian countries, still in many ways constitutes a "least likely scenario" for class-based disparities in media practices (see also Sivertsen, 2023). Sweden is still relatively egalitarian, and the access to certain media and communications is nearly universal. The media practices that we deal with in this chapter include how people use their smartphones, how they connect to the public sphere via news consumption, and the gratifications they seek from watching television. Most adult citizens in

Western democracies (including Sweden) dedicate at least some portion of their everyday lives to these media practices. Nine out of ten Swedes use the internet on a daily basis (Internetstiftelsen, 2021), 97 percent have access to a smartphone, and 89 percent of the population is reached by either streamed or linear television on a regular day (Ohlsson, 2023). Additionally, more than 70 percent of Swedes are exposed to national news more than three days per week (SOM, 2022). Given this backdrop, one may wonder how a Bourdieusian study of the relationship between media practices and social inequality would fare in the Swedish context. We first turn to news consumption.

Quality news in the social space

In journalism studies and political communication scholarship, and in society at large, journalism in democratic societies is framed as a key conduit between citizens and the political system – a collective good (Allern & Pollack, 2019). According to the prevailing discourse on the role and function of journalism in society, it is the duty of citizens to stay updated on current affairs in order to enact their rights as citizens in a democracy (McCombs & Poindexter, 1983). By and large, this view is shared by Swedish citizens, as 88 percent of the adult population agree that it is their duty as citizens to stay updated on the news (Bergström, 2016: 381). Thus, in the space of lifestyles, the consumption of the "quality press" finds itself in close proximity to other canonized and institutionalized cultural goods (Lindell, 2018; Sivertsen, 2023). To speak with MCA, variables measuring such tastes tend to "catch" the same individuals, that is, agents in the dominant region in the social space. But, as indicated by the fact that the vast majority of Swedes considers it a duty to stay updated on the news, news consumption tends to be collectively recognized. In this sense, the differences between social groups lie perhaps not so much in the extent to which people legitimize certain cultural goods but rather in the degree to which they know it and the ways in which they position themselves in relation to it (Bourdieu, 1984: 318).

In Figure 4.1 a number of media practices are projected as supplementary variables into a statistical representation of the Swedish class structure (the social space) studied in Figure 3.2, Chapter 3 (for details on significance tests for the supplementary categories, see Table 4.1). In this figure the vertical axis captures the principle of capital volume (high [top]/low [bottom]) while the horizontal axis describes oppositions between different capital endowments (cultural capital [left-hand side] vs. economic capital [right-hand side]). The active variables used to construct the space (capital endowments) are invisible and focus is put on the supplementary variables projected onto the space without affecting its structure (media practices). In terms of statistically notable distributions of variable categories, we observe the daily consumption of the "quality newspapers" (*Dagens Nyheter* and *Svenska Dagbladet*) located at about .5 deviations upwards from the center of the space, indicating that

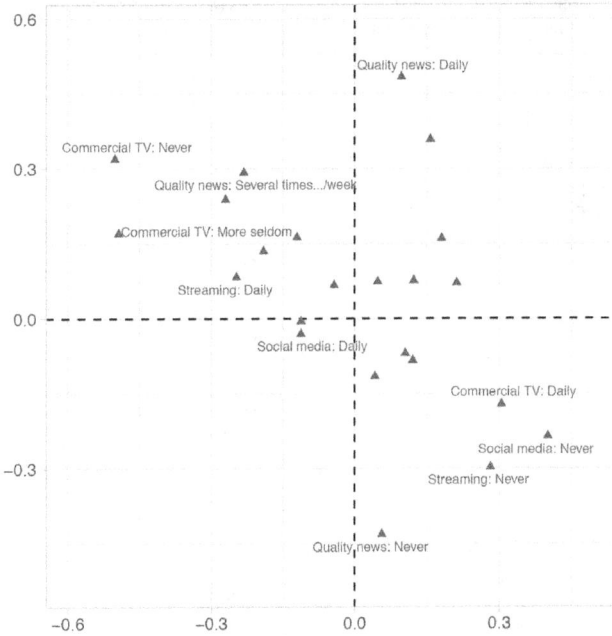

Figure 4.1 Media practices in the social space. Cloud of categories (supplementary variables)

it is tied to positions of relative privilege (high volumes of both economic and cultural capital). These two outlets, originally local newspapers in the Stockholm area, address a national audience (although they are frequently accused of being Stockholm-biased) and are characterized by extensive coverage of national and international affairs and cultural debate (Gustafsson & Rydén, 2010). The distribution of the frequency of consumption of the quality press roughly follows the vertical axis in the space, reaching its lowest level ("never") at about .5 deviations downwards from the center of the space (indicating that the lack of social resources corresponds to abstaining from the quality press). Lindell and Hovden (2018) uncovered a similar pattern in the taste for international news coverage where the lower classes' abstention from this genre was contrasted by the deep engagement in world affairs among people with high volumes of both economic and cultural capital.

The consumption of the most "serious" and in-depth (culturally, politically, and economically) newspapers follows the capital volume hierarchy closely. The choice of newspaper is, in the words of Prieur and colleagues, "a strong marker of social position" (2008: 61). Certain news outlets and genres, however, particularly the tabloid paper *Aftonbladet* and local news (not shown

Table 4.1 V-test for supplementary variable categories (media use) in relation to dimensions 1 and 2 in Figure 4.1

Variable category	Dimension 1	Dimension 2
Social media: Daily	−6.519	−1.774
Social media: Several times/week	1.890	1.173
Social media: Weekly	1.690	3.844
Social media: Monthly/more seldom	2.030	1.804
Social media: Never	5.373	−3.153
Commercial TV: Daily	9.605	−5.410
Commercial TV: Several times/week	2.674	−1.845
Commercial TV: Weekly	−3.609	2.564
Commercial TV: Monthly	−3.343	2.952
Commercial TV: More seldom	−6.901	2.383
Commercial TV: Never	−5.560	3.539
Quality news: Daily	2.045	10.122
Quality news: Several times/week	−3.042	3.838
Quality news: Weekly	−1.663	2.245
Quality news: Monthly	−1.629	−0.080
Quality news: More seldom	1.025	−2.764
Quality news: Never	1.392	−10.556
Streaming: Daily	−6.339	2.145
Streaming: Several times/week	−1.035	1.623
Streaming: Weekly	0.852	1.317
Streaming: Monthly	2.408	0.816
Streaming: More seldom	1.375	−0.907
Streaming: Never	5.268	−5.574

Note: Values that indicate statistically significant correspondences (−2 to 2) have been bolded.

in Figure 4.1), reach widely into Swedish society. By contrast, the quality newspapers cater to people with specific *qualities* that are granted by the fact that these social agents, by virtue of their positions of relative privilege, have stakes in the field of power. Financial investments correspond to "investments" in financial news coverage, political influence or interests presuppose taking part in or being part of political debates, and stakes in academic, intellectual, or cultural fields reflect in the inclination to engage in culture sections of the quality press:

> Like "difficult" art as opposed to "facile" art, or eroticism as opposed to pornography, the so-called quality newspapers call for a relation to the object implying the affirmation of a distance from the object which is the affirmation of a power over the object and also of the dignity of the subject. They give the reader much more than the "personal" opinions he needs; they acknowledge his dignity as a political subject capable of being, if not a subject of history, then at least the subject of a discourse on history.
>
> (Bourdieu, 1984: 446)

So far, we have explored news consumption only in regard to the "vertical" stratification of the social world. Studies have nonetheless shown that news preferences are also linked to positions tied to various capital endowments and the second principle of social differentiation. For instance, the taste for culture news is overrepresented in the cultural factions of the dominant social groups. This faction is also prone to tune in to the news coverage and in-depth journalistic broadcasts on public service radio P1 and to the canonized music culture (classical music, jazz) on P2. By contrast, the financial news is considered important by members of the economic middle class (Lindell, 2018). These patterns emerge in (in almost comical correspondence with the statistical associations in MCA research) focus group interviews with young people from different social origins. The cultural inheritors in university-preparatory upper-secondary schools, the sons and daughters of university teachers, doctors, and librarians, stress the importance of the news for "knowing where one stands" and as crucial for their ability to construct an opinion. Their peers in the economic faction of the social space, where parents hold jobs in the private sector (banking, real estate, etc.), instead stress the importance of "knowing the exchange rate of the dollar" (Lindell & Sartoretto, 2018).

In sum, the ways in which people, by way of their news repertoires, connect to the public sphere are socially differentiated (see also Hovden, 2023; Sivertsen, 2023). The Bourdieusian view on the social space and the distribution of news repertoires in that space reveal that news consumption is embedded in deep-seated social structures, and that people tend to reproduce their positions in their (public) lifestyles. Contrary to studies on the associations between "socio-economic status" (which aggregates cultural and economic capital and even occupations) and news consumption, the Bourdieusian approach reveals discrepancies between different forms of capital, and places news repertoires in relation to a broader space of lifestyles.

Uses of the smartphone in the social space

Nine out of ten Swedes have access to a smartphone. However, when we project various uses of the smartphone into the social space, we can identify patterns pertaining to the social regularities uncovered by Bourdieusian scholarship. The present analyses are based on an online survey administered by Kantar-Sifo in 2021 (n = 2401). In further exploring the patterns regarding news preferences, Figure 4.2 illustrates the frequencies at which people across the social space rely on their smartphones to access the coverage of cultural issues in the news. In this model of the social space, the horizontal axis taps into discrepancies in terms of access to either cultural capital (right) or economic capital (left). The vertical axis resembles the capital volume principle of differentiation (high volumes at the top, low volumes in the bottom). While the inclination to access culture news is significantly connected (in terms of the V-test) to both axes, the categories' distances from the center of the space

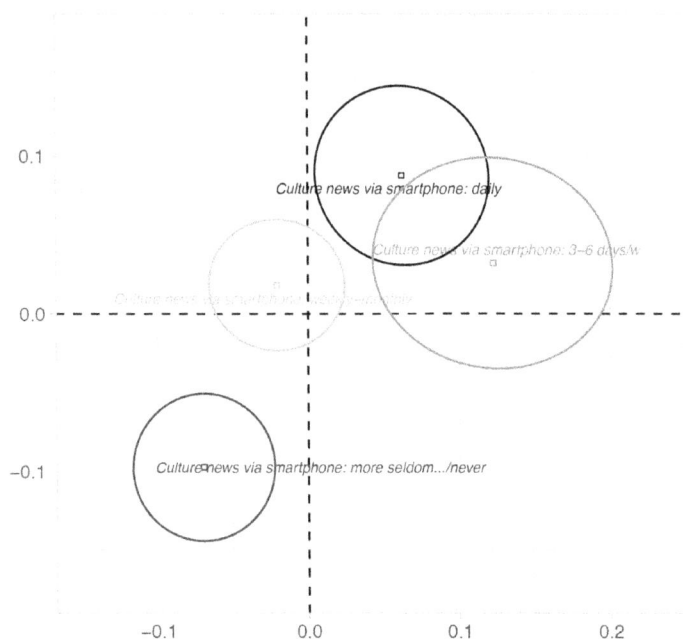

Figure 4.2 "Culture news via smartphones" in the social space. Confidence ellipses

are small. While the general taste for culture news is more clearly differentiated in the social space (Lindell, 2018), accessing this type of news through
mobile technology seems less of a distinctive practice. The (weak) associations nonetheless illustrate a diagonal pattern where the infrequent consumption of culture news is found in segments that are defined primarily by their
lack of capital, particularly cultural capital, and where regular consumption is
found among those rich in cultural capital. The confidence ellipses reveal that
these categories tend to catch different individuals (Figure 4.2). The opposite
distribution is found in the study of the frequency at which people shop online
(Lindell & Hovden, 2018). While the consumption of cultural news starts at
low levels in regions of the social space characterized by the lack of cultural
capital and is the highest among the culturally initiated classes, the inclination
to buy various products online is the lowest among agents lacking economic
capital and the highest among the affluent (Lindell & Hovden, 2018). These
two reverse patterns in the media practices of different social groups further
highlight the homologous relationship between the space of media practices
and the social space.

Figure 4.3 turns to a different kind of research question dealing with
"transmedia work" (Fast & Jansson, 2019), as focus is put on the inclination

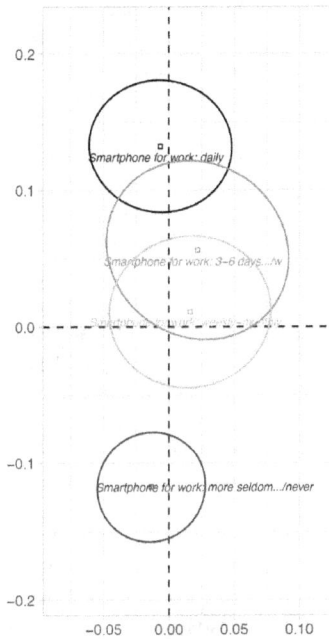

Figure 4.3 "Smartphones at work" in the social space. Confidence ellipses

to rely on the smartphone in working life. Above all, studying this map is an exercise in reflexivity on the part of the researcher, as the limits of a narrow Bourdieu-inspired endeavor are disclosed. We may nonetheless conclude that although the categories are located close to the center of the space, their positions are significantly related to the capital volume axis (indicated by V-tests not shown here due to limited space). As such, one would be inclined to posit that this manifestation of "transmedia work" follows the vertical hierarchy in the social space, which by extension suggests that white-collar and middle-class groups whose positions are marked by access to both economic and cultural capital are more likely to rely on the smartphone in their jobs. This is highlighted by the confidence ellipses, particularly the relatively isolated category of infrequent uses of the smartphone at work, which is located at a more precarious position in the space. An initial analysis thus suggests that relying on the smartphone at work constitutes the kind of "luxury problem" tied first and foremost to the middle- and upper-class professions (Fast & Jansson, 2019: 2).

The model, however, does not seem fit for the research question at hand, which concerns the extent to which work and professional life is saturated by mobile media. A research question dealing with how people rely on various media technologies, such as the smartphone, in their working life would be better off starting in the "reciprocal approach", in the construction of a "space of smartphone uses" (as others have done when studying the space of media use: see Hovden & Rosenlund, 2021; Purhonen et al. 2021; Sivertsen, 2023). In the second step, occupational (and other demographical) categories would be projected into that space. Another problem pertains to the fact that the model and the results risk obscuring the increasingly prevalent forms of "enforced transmedia work" and that the most precarious workers of digital modernity, the gig-workers, "are required to possess a smartphone and to be continuously connected not to miss any opportunities" (Fast & Jansson, 2019: 134–135). On the one hand, this could explain the small distances in the space, indicating that the intense use of smartphones at work captures both the gig-workers constantly monitoring apps in search for gigs and university teachers and corporate executives using their smartphones to answer emails, read news, and micro-manage careers on digital platforms. On the other hand, the same pattern might reveal the limits of the survey method as such, highlighting the challenge in reaching precarious social groups. This kind of methodological middle-class bias is manifested not only in survey researchers' difficulties reaching disadvantaged social groups, but also in that the questionnaires, which are oftentimes created from social positions of relative privilege and "scholastic" visions on the social world, tend to fail to properly account for "illegitimate" lifestyles (Heikkilä, 2021).

With this example, we are reminded about the open-ended and empirically oriented principles of the Bourdieusian approach that sometimes get lost in ambitions to uncover the principles Bourdieu laid out 30 or 40 years ago. Sometimes there are limited prospects to stubbornly insisting on starting the analysis in the social space. In cases where the research question deals with a particular form of media practice, it is advised to instead start in the *object of study* (e.g., the space of smartphone uses), rather than in the distributions of economic and cultural capital (the social space).

Distinctive modes of watching television

Watching television is, like in many countries, a near universal practice in Sweden, and still constitutes the most common form of media use in the population. In media scholars' response to Bourdieu's *Distinction*, the democratizing potential of the medium has been highlighted (Garnham, 1993), suggesting that television would break down the lifestyle hierarchies documented in other domains of culture consumption. In the Bourdieusian study of television practices, we nonetheless empirically ask about the extent to which the durable systems of classification (habitus) engender different modes of viewing among social groups characterized by different access to various forms of capital. This, of course, implies a break with one of the dominant strands in the research of media use – the uses and gratification approach – which posits that the gratifications people seek hinge on individual abilities and motivations rather than social structures. Since we focus on the "social topology" (Bourdieu, 1989) of social positions and television preferences, our approach also contrasts, and supplements, the ethnographic approach to media reception endorsed within cultural studies.

Figure 4.1, which constituted the basis from which we analyzed the social differentiation pertaining to the consumption of quality news, reveals another notable association: the (dis)taste for commercially produced television. The rejection of commercial television channels is found among cultural middle-class fractions (over .5 deviations to the west on the composition axis and about .3 deviations to the north). The fact that the categories of this variable are distributed diagonally across the space, starting at high levels among social groups lacking cultural capital and ending in the outright rejection amongst the culturally rich middle-class groups, reveals traces of a homologous relationship between the field of cultural production and the field of consumption (the social space). The field of cultural production is characterized by an opposition between "pure" art (art for art's sake) and commercial production aimed at wide audiences (Bourdieu, 1996; see Chapter 5). Evidently, this broad opposition inscribed in the logics of the "supply side" is reflected in the social positions on the "demand side", that is, in the preferences among different television audiences.

Moving deeper into the Bourdieusian analysis of television preferences, we turn to the gratifications that people seek from watching television. More specifically, using data from a survey conducted in 2023 (n = 2,403), focus is put on what people value when watching television. In this representation of the social space, the horizontal axis separates low volumes of capital (left) from high volumes of capital (right), whereas the vertical axis separates individuals in terms of the structure of their capital (high cultural capital at the bottom, high economic capital at the top). Although the associations between the axes and television preferences are generally weak (not shown in Figure 4.4), they closely follow the logics described by previous research, where "demanding" modes of consumption correspond to the symbolic mastery implied in having access to cultural capital, and where "expensive" tastes (such as big television sets) correspond to positions of relative economic affluence (see also Flemmen et al., 2018; Atkinson, 2022). In this sense, a culturally initiated middle-class position is characterized by a distaste toward reality-based, light-hearted domestic productions. This group also watches less television compared to other groups (Bennett et al., 2009) and is drawn to aesthetically refined shows that provide new perspectives (Hovden & Rosenlund, 2021; Krolo et al., 2023). As a case in point, Figure 4.4 shows the distribution of variable categories measuring the extent to which respondents agree that "good" television experiences are defined by the degree to which a given show is aesthetically appealing. By contrast, respondents with low levels of capital who subsequently lack the habitus required to appreciate the "legitimate culture"

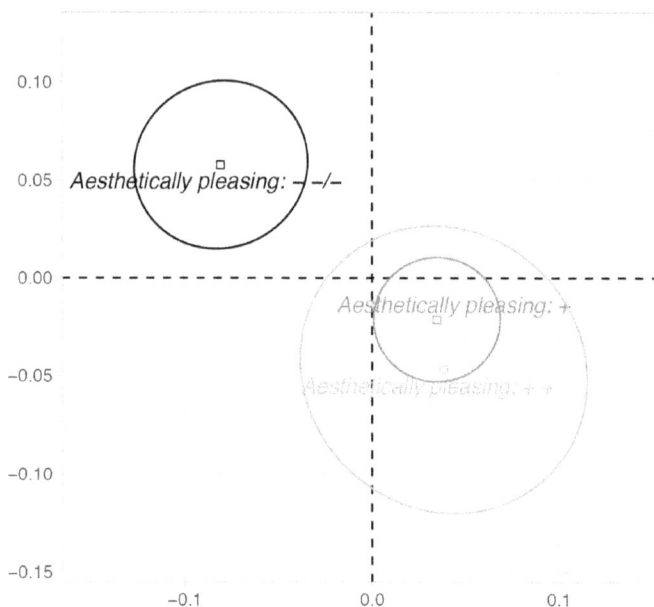

Figure 4.4 "Watching television should be aesthetically appealing" in the social space. Confidence ellipses

in a "legitimate manner" (Bourdieu, 1984: 87) value the audio-visual experience of watching television more than the content in itself. They also prefer reality-based shows produced in the Swedish language and spend significant amounts of time watching television (not illustrated in figure).

Conclusion

This chapter has illustrated a key facet in Bourdieusian media studies: the study of the media practices that people devote significant parts of their everyday lives to. Framed as part of broader lifestyles rooted in particular social conditions and positions, people's media practices and media repertoires have been shown to reflect and reproduce social positions. The clearest example in this chapter is found in the example of the taste for quality newspapers, which is widespread in the upper echelons of the social space and gradually less common as we move downward along the capital volume axis. For most media researchers, this is a worrying observation, as the consumption of news is an important pillar in the exercise of citizenship and political participation in democratic societies. News consumption is, in other words, not a lifestyle manifestation among others (like visits to the theater or tastes in film and music) and as such it deserves the attention of MCA-oriented media researchers (Lindell, 2018; Hovden, 2023; Sivertsen, 2023).

Both capital volume and capital composition matter in the formation of media practices. In this chapter we have seen that television shows and news outlets that presuppose symbolic mastery and the ability to decipher specific cultural codes and the rejection of commercial television channels correspond to positions characterized by high volumes of capital, particularly in its cultural form. Materialist and expensive practices reflect economic affluence. Thus, even in the "egalitarian" and highly digitalized context of Sweden, media practices follow social hierarchies (see also Hjellbrekke et al., 2015). However, the chapter has also discussed the limits to the Bourdieusian method, in particular the tendency to begin any analysis in the social space. In some cases, this is a blunt and indirect way of studying media practices. An alternative is to rely on the "reciprocal approach" (Rosenlund, 2015) and begin the analysis in the space of media use instead of in the system of class relations (e.g., Hovden & Rosenlund, 2021; Purhonen et al., 2021; Sivertsen, 2023).

Additional critique includes the argument that the approach puts too much focus on the original conceptions of the social space as structured by volume and composition of capital, oftentimes at the expense of age (Glevarec & Cibois, 2021). While this chapter shows that when methodological focus is put on people's capital endowments, we tend to end up in the structure of the social space similar to the one Bourdieu (1984) described. This model, and the view on the social world it promotes (according to which habitus explains practice), nonetheless obscures other factors that can be understood to structure the social space in general and media practices in particular (de Saint Martin, 2015; Glevarec & Cibois, 2021). Age, gender, and ethnicity are three such factors that can be included either as active variables in the construction of the social space, or as supplementary variables in the study of symbolic spaces (such as the space of media practices). Alternatively, the social space can be constructed around one specific generation, or various measures can be taken to account for the ways in which age and cultural history structure tastes and lifestyles (Glevarec & Cibois, 2021). A particular focus on gender differences in both the social space (distribution of capitals) and the space of lifestyles is warranted in societies (including Sweden) where men and women are, sociologically speaking, drifting further and further apart (e.g., in terms of women dominance in educational attainment and consumption of canonized culture as well as increased political polarization between genders) (*Financial Times*, 2024). Furthermore, the analysis of the social spaces in welfare states with extensive public sectors (such as Sweden) can include the employment sector (public versus private) as an active variable, as it captures local peculiarities in the capital composition dynamic (Broady, 2001), whereas the analysis of other societies might warrant including military training and ranks (Bühlmann et al., 2013). Transnationalization suggests including "cosmopolitan capital" as a facet of cultural capital (e.g., Bühlmann et al., 2013; Lindell, 2018). This highlights the task of understanding the (g)local characteristics of the social space in question. This is also to say that contemporary spaces of differentiation and the production of divergent position-takings call for a break with the strict homology thesis and the focus on class habitus as the main structuring factor for practices and preferences. The social space can thus be conceptualized anew through the lens of the *plural habitus*, a concept that recognizes that actors are multi-socialized and multi-determined (Hadas, 2022: 94; see also Lahire, 2015).

This chapter has illustrated a Bourdieusian approach to the study of media use. The examples in this chapter are far from exhaustive. Recent studies have, for example, asked about the extent to which correspondences between media practices and social positions translate into symbolic violence, whereby agents at lower social positions (where "illegitimate" tastes are more pronounced) would stigmatize their own tastes (Lindell, 2022). Results suggest, contrary to the view that the lower classes impose symbolic violence upon themselves (Bourdieu, 1984), that it is agents at emerging cultural middle-class positions (who are invested in "cultural" fields) that display anxious attitudes to their own media practices. Part of the explanation is that algorithmically curated media repertoires limit the reach of the "legitimate" culture, allowing the formation of "audience islands" and alternative classification systems in lower positions in the social space (Lindell & Hovden, 2018; Lindell, 2022).

Whatever media practices or media repertoires a researcher is interested in, the Bourdieusian approach and the method of MCA offer useful tools for empirical research. It is, for instance, perfectly possible to study political participation, (reasons for) news avoidance, media trust, attitudes toward AI or media policy suggestions, mediatized cultural participation, and so on in the Bourdieusian way. A key take-away from this chapter is that we need to carefully choose the method of approach (either the social space approach or the reciprocal approach) and consider the various ways in which the focus on capital endowments can be supplemented by including in the analysis other important factors that shape media practices, such as age, ethnicity, and gender.

References

Allern, S., & Pollack, E. (2019). Journalism as a public good: A Scandinavian perspective. *Journalism*, *20*(11), 1423–1439.

Anderson, B. (1983). *Imagined communities: Reflections on the origins and spread of nationalism*. London: Verso.

Atkinson, W. (2022). The US space of lifestyles and its homologies. *Sociological Perspectives*, *65*(6), 1060–1080.

Baeten, G., Berg, L., & Lund Hansen, A. (2015). Introduction: Neoliberalism and post-welfare Nordic states in transition. *Geografiska Annaler: Series B, Human Geography*, *97*(3), 209–212.

Bengtsson, S. (2015). Digital distinctions: Mechanisms of difference in digital media use. *MedieKultur: Journal of Media and Communication Research, 31*(58), 30–48.

Bennett, T., Savage, M., Silva, E., Warde, A., Gayo-Cal, M., & Wright, D. (2009). *Culture, class, distinction.* London: Routledge.

Bergström, A. (2016). Nyheter – både plikt och nöje [News – both duty and pleasure]. In J. Ohlsson, H. Oscarsson, & M. Solevid (Eds.), *Ekvilibrium* (pp. 377–388). Göteborg: Göteborgs universitet, SOM-institutet.

Bolin, G. (2011). *Value and the media: Cultural production and consumption in digital markets.* Farnham, Surrey: Ashgate.

Börjesson, M. (2016). ANFÖRANDE: Sociala kartor över utbildningslandskapet: Installationsföreläsning, professuren i utbildningssociologi vid Uppsala universitet, 11 november 2015. *Sociologisk forskning, 53*(4), 421–436.

Bourdieu, P. (1984). *Distinction: A social critique of the judgement of taste.* New York: Routledge.

Bourdieu, P. (1989). Social space and symbolic power. *Sociological Theory, 7*(1), 14–25.

Bourdieu, P. (1990). *The logic of practice.* Stanford, CA: Stanford University Press.

Bourdieu, P. (1991). *Language and symbolic power.* Cambridge: Polity.

Bourdieu, P. (1996). *The rules of art: Genesis and structure of the literary field.* Cambridge: Polity.

Bourdieu, P. (2000). *Pascalian meditations.* Cambridge: Polity.

Bourdieu, P. (2013). Symbolic capital and social classes. *Journal of Classical Sociology, 13*(2), 292–302.

Broady, D. (2001). What is cultural capital? Comments on Lennart Rosenlund's *Social Structures and Change. Sosiologisk Årbok/Yearbook of Sociology, 6*(2), 45–59.

Brüggemann, M., Engesser, S., Büchel, F., Humprecht, E., & Castro, L. (2014). Hallin and Mancini revisited: Four empirical types of Western media systems. *Journal of Communication, 64*(6), 1037–1065.

Bühlmann, F., David, T., & Mach, A. (2013). Cosmopolitan capital and the internationalization of the field of business elites: Evidence from the Swiss case. *Cultural Sociology, 7*(2), 211–229.

Coulangeon, P., & Duval, J. (Eds.). (2015). *The Routledge companion to Bourdieu's Distinction.* London, New York: Routledge.

Couldry, N. (2003). Media meta-capital: Extending the range of Bourdieu's field theory. *Theory and Society, 32*, 653–677.

Couldry, N. (2004). Theorising media as practice. *Social Semiotics, 14*(2), 115–132.

Cvetičanin, P., Pereira, L. P., Petrić, M., Tomić-Koludrović, I., Lebaron, F., & Zdravković, Ž. (2024). Cultural practices and socio-digital inequalities in Europe: Towards a unified research framework in cultural participation studies. *Cultural Sociology*, 17499755231222520.

de Saint Martin, M. (2015). From "Anatomie du gout" to La Distinction: Attempting to construct the social space: Some markers for the history of research. In P. Coulangeon & J. Duval (Eds.), *The Routledge companion to Bourdieu's Distinction* (pp. 15–28). London, New York: Routledge.

Fast, K., & Jansson, A. (2019). *Transmedia work: Privilege and precariousness in digital modernity.* London, New York: Routledge.

Financial Times. (2024). A new global gender divide is emerging. https://www.ft.com/content/29fd9b5c-2f35-41bf-9d4c-994db4e12998. Accessed 1 March 2024.

Flemmen, M., Jarness, V., & Rosenlund, L. (2018). Social space and cultural class divisions: The forms of capital and contemporary lifestyle differentiation. *The British Journal of Sociology, 69*(1), 124–153.

Garnham, N. (1993). Bourdieu, the cultural arbitrary, and television. In C. Calhoun, E. LiPuma, & M. Postone (Eds.), *Bourdieu: Critical perspectives* (pp. 178–192). Cambridge: Polity.

Gaw, F. (2022). Algorithmic logics and the construction of cultural taste of the Netflix recommender system. *Media, Culture & Society, 44*(4), 706–725.

Glevarec, H., & Cibois, P. (2021). Structure and historicity of cultural tastes. Uses of multiple correspondence analysis and sociological theory on age: The case of music and movies. *Cultural Sociology, 15*(2), 271–291.

Gustafsson, K. E., & Rydén, P. (2010). *A history of the press in Sweden.* Gothenburg: Nordicom.

Hadas, M. (2022). *Outlines of a theory of plural habitus: Bourdieu revisited.* London: Routledge.

Hasebrink, U., & Popp, J. (2006). Media repertoires as a result of selective media use. A conceptual approach to the analysis of patterns of exposure. *Communications, 31*, 369–287.

Heikkilä, R. (2021). The slippery slope of cultural non-participation: Orientations of participation among the potentially passive. *European Journal of Cultural Studies, 24*(1), 202–219.

Hjarvard, S. (2013). *The mediatization of culture and society.* New York: Routledge.

Hjellbrekke, J., Jarness, V., & Korsnes, O. (2015). Cultural distinctions in an "egalitarian" society. In P. Coulangeon & J. Duval (Eds.), *The Routledge companion to Bourdieu's Distinction* (pp. 187–206). London, New York: Routledge.

Hovden, J. F. (2023). Worlds apart. On class structuration of citizens' political and public attention and engagement in an egalitarian society. *European Journal of Cultural and Political Sociology, 10*(2), 209–232.

Hovden, J. F., & Moe, H. (2017). A sociocultural approach to study public connection across and beyond media: The example of Norway. *Convergence, 23*(4), 391–408.

Hovden, J. F., & Rosenlund, L. (2021). Class and everyday media use: A case study from Norway. *Nordicom Review, 42*(S3), 129–149.

Internetstiftelsen. (2021). Svenskarna och internet 2021 [The Swedes and Internet 2021]. Available at https://svenskarnaochinternet.se/app/uploads/2021/09/internetstiftelsen-svenskarna-och-internet-2021.pdf.

Jakobsson, P., Lindell, J., & Stiernstedt, F. (2021). A neoliberal media welfare state? The Swedish media system in transformation. *Javnost – The Public, 28*(4), 375–390.

Jansson, A. (2002). The mediatization of consumption: Towards an analytical framework of image culture. *Journal of Consumer Culture, 2*(1), 5–31.

Kalogeropoulos, A., & Nielsen, R. (2018). *Social inequalities in news consumption* [Fact sheet]. Reuter's Institute.

Krolo, K., Tonković, Ž., & Vozab, D. (2023). Between breaking bad and big brother: Social class and television preferences in Croatia. *Sociological Research Online,* 13607804231207253.

Lahire, B. (2015). Culture at the level of the individual: Challenging transferability. In P. Coulangeon & J. Duval (Eds.), *The Routledge companion to Bourdieu's Distinction* (pp. 109–118). London, New York: Routledge.

Leguina, A., & Downey, J. (2021). Getting things done: Inequalities, internet use and everyday life. *New Media & Society*, *23*(7), 1824–1849.

Lindell, J. (2018). *Distinction* recapped: Digital news repertoires in the class structure. *New Media & Society*, *20*(8), 3029–3049.

Lindell, J. (2022). Symbolic violence and the social space: Self-imposing the mark of disgrace? *Cultural Sociology*, *16*(3), 379–401.

Lindell, J. (forthcoming). Digital journalism and "radical audience studies": Toward a cultural sociology of news use. In S. Banjac, D. Cheruiyot, S. Eldridge, & J. Swart (Eds.), *Routledge companion to digital journalism studies* (2nd ed.). London: Routledge.

Lindell, J., & Hovden, J. F. (2018). Distinctions in the media welfare state: Audience fragmentation in post-egalitarian Sweden. *Media, Culture & Society*, *40*(5), 639–655.

Lindell, J., & Sartoretto, P. (2018). Young people, class and the news: Distinction, socialization and moral sentiments. *Journalism Studies*, *19*(14), 2042–2061.

Lindell, J., Jansson, A., & Fast, K. (2022). I'm here! Conspicuous geomedia practices and the reproduction of social positions on social media. *Information, Communication & Society*, *25*(14), 2063–2082.

Lundahl, O. (2022). Algorithmic meta-capital: Bourdieusian analysis of social power through algorithms in media consumption. *Information, Communication & Society*, *25*(10), 1440–1455.

Madianou, M. (2009). Audience reception and news in everyday life. In K. Wahl-Jorgensen & T. Hanitzsch (Eds.), *The handbook of journalism studies* (pp. 325–337). London, New York: Routledge.

McCombs, M., & Poindexter, P. (1983). The duty to keep informed: News exposure and civic obligation. *Journal of Communication*, *33*(2), 88–96.

Mihelj, S., Leguina, A., & Downey, J. (2019). Culture is digital: Cultural participation, diversity and the digital divide. *New Media & Society*, *21*(7), 1465–1485.

Neveu, E. (2005). Bourdieu, the Frankfurt school, and cultural studies: On some misunderstandings. In R. Benson & E. Neveu (Eds.), *Bourdieu and the journalistic field* (pp. 195–213). Cambridge: Polity.

Ohlsson, J. (Ed.). (2023). *Mediebarometern 2022*. Gothenburg: Nordicom.

Prieur, A., Rosenlund, L., & Skjott-Larsen, J. (2008). Cultural capital today: A case study from Denmark. *Poetics*, *36*(1), 45–71.

Prior, M. (2007). *Post-broadcast democracy: How media choice increases inequality in political involvement and polarizes elections*. Cambridge: Cambridge University Press.

Purhonen, S., Leguina, A., & Heikkilä, R. (2021). The space of media usage in Finland, 2007 and 2018: The impact of online activities on its structure and its association with sociopolitical divisions. *Nordicom Review*, *42*(s3), 111–128.

Rosenlund, L. (2015). Working with Distinction: Scandinavian experiences. In P. Coulangeon & J. Duval (Eds.), *The Routledge companion to Bourdieu's Distinction* (pp. 157–186). London, New York: Routledge.

Sapiro, G. (2015). The international career of Distinction. In P. Coulangeon & J. Duval (Eds.), *The Routledge companion to Bourdieu's Distinction* (pp. 29–42). London: Routledge.

Schrøder, K. C. (2011). Audiences are inherently cross-media: Audience studies and the cross-media challenge. *Communication Management Quarterly*, *18*(6), 5–27.

Sivertsen, M. F. (2023). Stratified public connections—beyond the taste for news? *Journalism Studies*, 1–21.

SOM. (2022). *Svenska tender 1986–2022* [Swedish trends 1986–2022]. Göteborg: SOM-institutet.

Syvertsen, T., Enli, G., Mjos, O., & Moe, H. (2014). *The media welfare state: Nordic media in the digital era.* Ann Arbor: University of Michigan Press.

Therborn, G. (2020). Sweden's turn to economic inequality, 1982–2019. *Structural Change and Economic Dynamics, 52*, 159–166.

Tichenor, J. P., Donohue, G. A., & Olien, C. N. (1970). Mass media flow and differential growth in knowledge. *The Public Opinion Quarterly, 34*(2), 159–170.

5 Fields of media and cultural production

Introduction

The Bourdieusian approach is, as shown in the previous chapter, a powerful alternative to the established research traditions within which media and communication scholars study "users" and "audiences" of the media. By way of a social topology, realized by the use of multiple correspondence analysis (MCA), media practices were analyzed in the social terrain of domination and subordination and in relation to broader lifestyles. This approach can with equal force be applied to the study of the specific fields of media and cultural production which, by virtue of their capacity to construct specific visions of the social world, function as cultural intermediaries, or tastemakers, in the social space. As will be shown in this chapter, and as both Willig (2016) and Slaatta (2016) have argued, the Bourdieusian view offers something different to media production studies, which has favored on-site observations and qualitative interviews. This chapter focuses on three different fields: the journalistic field, the field of television production, and the academic field of media and communication studies. MCA is used in the empirical study of the latter two. While the study of television production draws on survey data, the exploration of the academic field illustrates the prosopographic method. These fields have in common the symbolic power of representing, framing, and interpreting the social world, but agents do so from different positions. In the bird's-eye view, these fields are sub-fields within the broader field of cultural production. They are populated by agents with stakes in the game within the respective fields, who recognize the legitimacy in the struggles of the game and have incorporated its rules in their dispositions. With this chapter, we thus move away from the analysis of the social space (and the space of lifestyles) and turn instead to another facet of field theory: field analysis.

In applying field theory to the analysis of media production, media scholars frequently turn to *On Television and Journalism* (Bourdieu, 1998), a short book meant for public debate on the dangers stemming from the increasingly heteronomous (commercialized) journalistic field's capacity to impose its logics on other fields of cultural production (such as the academic field).

DOI: 10.4324/9781003364245-5

While this book certainly has its merits, it is in *The Rules of Art* (1996) that Bourdieu spells out his theory of fields at length. As such, this book is given special attention in this chapter. I begin, however, by unearthing the main components in a Bourdieusian study of fields. This approach is supplemented with a recent attempt to clarify and operationalize a theory of fields (Fligstein & McAdam, 2012). The chapter then moves into the empirical study of the field of television production and the field of media and communication studies.

Fields

Modernity is a process of social differentiation marked by the division of labor and the subsequent formation of relatively autonomous social universes centered on specific competencies, interests, and struggles. In Europe, the 19th century witnessed the gradual separation of the art world, or the field of cultural production, from political and economic interests through the formation of the new position of "art for art's sake" (Bourdieu, 1996). The academic field, in turn, is occupied by social agents dedicated to the search for truth and the production of knowledge (the meaning of which being the site for field-internal struggles) whereas the journalistic field, through its gradual professionalization and institutionalization during the 20th century, accommodates agents invested in "reporting the world" to citizens (Bourdieu, 2005). These social microcosms are relatively autonomous social worlds in the sense that they (to varying degrees) are governed by their own logics. While increased politico-legal control of higher education and research (e.g., external ethics reviews and regulations, earmarked research funding, budget cuts, etc.) suggest that the academic field is becoming more heteronomous, it still to a comparably high degree abides by its own rules (*de facto* and *de jure*, as Bourdieu would put it). By contrast, the journalistic field is more heteronomous as it – to varying degrees, depending on the media system we are concerned with (Hallin & Mancini, 2004) – adapts to the economic field (e.g., audience ratings, advertisements), the political field (e.g., funding, censorship), and the technological field (e.g., innovation in journalistic practice) (Bourdieu, 1998; Champagne, 2005).

Fields are sites where specialists struggle over the specialty that is common to them. It is a network of objective positions wherein social agents are endowed with different amounts of the capital that is peculiar to the field: journalistic capital, academic capital, and so on. The objective positions in the field create a space of the possible and the impossible, and as such agents' positions tend to be reflected in position-takings (attitudes and practices) (Bourdieu, 2000). Like in his writings on the social space and lifestyles, Bourdieu (2000) holds that fields are marked by the homologous relationship between positions and dispositions, particularly within highly autonomous fields. While a field is populated by players who adopt different position-takings, which hinge on objective positions in the field, they share the belief and subsequent investment in the struggles of the field (*illusio*). Thus, the only true violation of the rules of the game is the refusal to play the game (Bourdieu, 2000: 256). In this sense, it is obvious that Bourdieu suggests that fields are characterized by inertia and reproduction, and that individual action within fields originates from a particular (socially molded) habitus rather than from rational choice or cynical strategy (Bourdieu, 2000). This, however, does not mean that field theory is insensitive to social change.

The Rules of Art is committed to analyzing the changes leading up to the formation of the current structure of the field of cultural production. Bourdieu (2000) is nonetheless somewhat ambivalent in regard to exactly how change occurs in fields. On the one hand, he posits that it is the non-consecrated avant-garde that is socially predisposed to revolutionize fields, because they would advance their positions by dethroning the consecrated elites. On the other hand, he forcefully argues that social agents from privileged backgrounds (that have granted them a distance from necessity) who have mastered the game of the field are the ones able to carve out new positions (like in how Flaubert, Manet, and Baudelaire created the "art for art's sake" position in the field of cultural production). In some respects, Bourdieu (2000) stresses exogenous change, such as the 1848 French Revolution or the expansion of the educational system (which brings both new producers and consumers to the literary field), whilst in most passages he highlights the endogenous origins of upheaval. In setting out to bring some clarity to the social origins of change in fields, Marantz and Cattani (2024) confirm Bourdieu's general observation that change is dependent on the structure and history of a field. Taking the example of the US television industry, they show that in times of stability in the field, high-status agents are more prone to produce innovative shows and, in a sense, to promote change in the field, whereas newcomers are more likely to innovate when the field is unstable.

The general principles of Bourdieusian sociology uncovered in Chapter 3 apply, of course, not only to the study of the social space and the space of lifestyles but also to the study of distinct fields. The approach is open-ended and puts high demands on empirical work, since the task is to (1) study the position of the given field in regard to other fields (particularly the field of power), (2) uncover the internal structure of the field, that is, its objective positions, and (3) explore the position-takings and the habitus of participants (Bourdieu, 2000: 312; see also Bourdieu & Wacquant, 1992: 104–105). In field analysis, theory is developed in tandem with empirical research, and focus is put on *relations* between positions in the field. This implies that, just like the categories of "high-brow" and "legitimate culture", the positions and position-takings within fields vary with both time and space (Bourdieu, 2000: 320), and that the researcher has to "construct" the field. As discussed in Chapter 2, a key concern among contemporary scholars regards globalization and the geographical reach of fields (Buchholz, 2016; Sapiro, 2018). For Bourdieu, the answer is both simple and difficult to answer (empirically): the field "stops" at the point where it does not have an effect, and a social agent exists in a field when he or she is affecting other players in it (2000: 327–328). In their attempt to spell out a general theory of fields, Fligstein and McAdam (2012) draw heavily on Bourdieu, and their approach shares his basic arguments. They hold, nonetheless, that Bourdieu fails to account for the collective aspects of action within fields, the relations between fields, as well as social change (2012: 24–25). Careful readers of *The Rules of Art* (Bourdieu, 1996) would probably disagree with Fligstein and McAdam's assessment (although it should be noted that they repeatedly refer to *The Rules of Art* as exempted from their critique). The extent to which Fligstein and McAdam present something new to the Bourdieusian approach can be (and has been) debated, and this is not the place to delve into this discussion. A key merit of *A Theory of Fields* is that it offers an accessible, pedagogical, and operational approach to the study of fields. For instance, their notion of "internal governance unit" (institutions wielding the power of consecration in fields, such as juries and committees) helps specify and label dynamics described by Bourdieu only in passing, and the concept of "socially skilled agents" supplements Bourdieu's analysis of individual agents that promote change. Their analysis of how fields come into being is particularly productive, especially the focus on states and technological innovation as facilitating the emergence of fields. Finally, and unlike Bourdieu (1996), Fligstein and McAdam hold that change does not usually originate from within fields but rather follows "exogenous shocks" such as the invasion of outside groups, change in neighboring fields, and macro-events like wars or economic depression (Fligstein & McAdam, 2012: 99). The empirical analyses of the field of television production and the field of media and communication studies presented below draw on both Bourdieu and Fligstein and McAdam, and show how the approaches can be used in tandem.

Box 5.1   The genesis and structure of the literary field: *The Rules of Art*

If *Distinction* is Bourdieu's central work on the consumption of culture, *The Rules of Art* is the headpiece of his works on the production of culture. It was published in French in 1992 and in English in 1996. Like Bourdieu's other works, the book is multifaceted. It includes a meticulous sociological reading of Gustave Flaubert's novel *Sentimental Education* (which, according to Bourdieu, describes the structure of the literary field that Flaubert found himself in) as well as an analysis of the genesis of the literary field and how it changed during the 19th century. It makes detours into the broader field of cultural production (including painting, academia, and journalism) and provides a general outline of the methodological principles of field analysis.

Before the revolution in 1848 and the following social upheavals, the French literary field was characterized by lack of autonomy, where the political field and the market both sanctioned and censored cultural production (Bourdieu, 2000: 94, 181). In the mid-19th century, however, the field was ripe for key agents in the literary field, whom Fligstein and McAdam (2012) would describe as "socially skilled", to bring about a structural transformation. The result of this process is the two-dimensional structure that we commonly associate with Bourdieu's take on the field of cultural production. In this structure, (1) autonomous, or "pure", production stands against industrial production, and (2) consecrated agents are pitted against newcomers and the non-consecrated avantgarde (Bourdieu, 1996: 124). The agents of change epitomize in the writers Gustave Flaubert (1821–1880) and Charles Baudelaire (1821–1867). Both were "unclassified bastards" (Bourdieu, 2000: 177, my translation) from privileged social backgrounds who also possessed the field-specific capitals and dispositions necessary to carve out a new position in the field. This new position would oppose both "social art" demanding that literature and art generally fill a moral, political, and social function and the bourgeois art adapted to audience demand and the prevailing political doxa (2000: 131). This new position was the position of "art for art's sake", and it made it so that the field of cultural production gradually came to revolve around a main opposition between "culture and money", that is, between autonomous art and commercial art (2000: 140, 190). The most autonomous region of the field ("art for art's sake") remained unaffected by external pressures (political censorship or economic interests), and cultural producers in this region sought legitimacy only amongst their peers. This part of the field turned into "the economic world reversed" wherein "the loser wins". Worldly achievements, including monetary success due to large audiences and editions, fame, and awards from conservative "internal governance units" (to speak with Fligstein & McAdam [2012]) constituted negative assets in this region in the field. If, however, the autonomous producers achieved worldly success, they did so after significant periods of time, compared to writers of commercial literature who were aligned with prevailing norms and audience demands.

Bourdieu (2000: 164) highlights how social agents from privileged backgrounds marked by a distance from necessity, who occupied ambivalent positions in the field (Flaubert, Manet, Baudelaire), were the ones bringing about social change. In all fields, Bourdieu (2000: 377) writes, the agents from the privileged positions have the habitus and the capital to "afford" to occupy the new positions (e.g., the avantgarde). He stresses, however, that there need to exist "structural gaps" in the field for change to take place, and thus that any transformation is always rooted in the existing structure of the field (2000: 147, 340). Like in other works, Bourdieu holds that positions in fields are homologous to dispositions held by agents. Marcel Duchamp, born and raised in the world of arts, moved about like a "fish in water" within the field of cultural production. By contrast, Léon Cladel, raised in the rural petty-bourgeoisie, tried out the Parisian bohemian life but eventually returned to the countryside to depict life there. The homology between positions and position-takings matters not only for individual trajectories in the field but also for transformations. In most cases, dominant and consecrated individuals seek to conserve the order of the field, because this order consecrated them. As such, the newcomers, the non-consecrated avantgarde (and also "unclassified bastards" such as Flaubert and Baudelaire) tend to be the ones predisposed to revolutionize fields.

The Rules of Art is Bourdieu's most complete introduction of the notion of field. It shows how field theory, as applied to the analysis of cultural production, avoids the reductionism involved in the internal deconstruction of the inner grammars of individual works of art and biographies of the "creative genius" that fail to account for the field-specific position that produced the author, and from which the author produced culture. It also avoids macro-leveled, external analyses that ignore the relational field-internal dynamics. The protagonist in the book is the field in itself, as a social fact, as Durkheim would put it. While the book describes the emergence of an autonomous field of cultural production, Bourdieu, in concluding, fears that the field is currently under threat from a number of external forces. The opposition between limited and autonomous production and industrial production is becoming more porous (Bourdieu, 2000: 480), not least due to what media scholars refer to as mediatization – the processes wherein other fields adapt to media logics (Hjarvard, 2008). Bourdieu ends his book by calling for a collective defense of autonomy in the field of cultural production, and it is from this premise that *On Television and Journalism* (Bourdieu, 1998) takes off.

In media and communication studies, the notion of field has been widely used by journalism scholars (Maares & Hanusch, 2022) in large parts thanks to Benson and Neveu's *Bourdieu and the Journalistic Field* (2005). The idea of the social field presented journalism scholars to a new unit of analysis – the universe of all players dedicated to the production of the news, including news organizations, individual journalists, and internal governance units such as systems for regulation (ombudsmen, bodies overlooking media ethics, etc.)

and consecration (educational institutions, associations granting awards, etc.) (Benson & Neveu, 2005; Champagne, 2005; Duval, 2005; Hovden, 2008).

In other realms of media and communication studies there have been complaints over the fact that Bourdieu almost exclusively focused on small-scale, autonomous production where the amounts of field-specific capitals are the highest (e.g., "art for art's sake") (Hesmondhalgh, 2006; Bolin, 2012). Indeed, when media scholars apply Bourdieu's outline of the structure of the French field of cultural production as a hypothesis to the study of contemporary fields of media production, they quickly encounter difficulties. One such difficulty is that large-scale media production is complex (Hesmondhalgh, 2006) since, for instance, commercialized media production does not necessarily aim at reaching the largest possible audience but rather the "right" target audience (Bolin, 2004, 2009). This directly breaks with Bourdieu's description of the French literary field in which autonomy is coupled with small-scale production and heteronomy with large-scale production. Another difficulty emerges when we turn to public service media – a paradoxical entity that is at the same time autonomous (from the market, and thus able to produce niche contents) and heteronomous in that it is sanctioned by the political field and oriented toward mass audiences (as per remits stating the mission to reach all citizens) (Bolin, 2004, 2012).

The affordances of digital media imply that media production is not necessarily constrained by logics and norms pertaining to specific fields (Lindell, 2015). Levina and Arriaga (2014) have argued that user-generated content takes place in distinct "online fields". For instance, while "content farms" producing short formats for distribution on social media platforms could be understood as positioned at the "far end of large-scale cultural production" (Mears, 2023: 1), most of these creators operate without adhering to the logics of particular fields of cultural production. Others have argued that digital and mobile media, which allow "anyone" to produce media content, can lead agents in the fields of media and cultural production to migrate to other fields (Solaroli, 2016). Reversely, social media stars, content creators, or "influencers" are sometimes recruited into organizations within existing fields, for instance to host popular television shows. In many contemporary cases, however, digital and non-institutionalized media production abides first and foremost by the logics of platforms (generating attention, views, clicks, likes, subscriptions, and followers) (Mears, 2023). As such, content creators compete with both agents in the social space ("ordinary internet users") and agents inside fields of cultural production (artists, writers, journalists, television producers, academics) in the global attention economy. One may thus ask about the extent to which the logics of the attention economy and social media platforms are rendering all fields of cultural production more heteronomous, and also more homogenous (Lindblom et al., 2022; Mears, 2023). The notions of "digital heteronomy" (Lindblom et al., 2022) and "algorithmic meta-capital" (Lundahl, 2022) describe this trend, as practices inside various fields of media and cultural production adopt strategies to gain algorithmic visibility (e.g., optimization of social media metrics and search engine results). By extension, this exogenous change process may promote metamorphosis in the field-specific capital (like the increased value of "virality capital" inside the journalistic field [Lindblom et al., 2022]).

Yet another challenge in using Bourdieu's outline as a ready-made hypothesis is the fact that media production is increasingly global in character. Although the persistence of domestic markets and regulations implies the continued existence of national fields of cultural production (Kuipers, 2015), researchers have to be open to the question regarding the extent to which a given field is transnational in its reach (Buchholz, 2016; Sapiro, 2018).

These challenges – the complexity of large-scale media production, the peculiar position of public service media, the global attention economy and platform logics, and the globalization of media markets – are factors that should be taken into account when a media researcher is "constructing the research object" in field analysis. In this vein one should keep in mind that Bourdieu's outline of the field of cultural production does not offer a ready-made hypothesis. Rather than expecting that the structure of the late 19th century French literary field (Bourdieu, 1996) should be perfectly replicated in a contemporary setting, the researcher has to construct the object, the theory calls for "practical implementation" (Bourdieu, 1991: 255).

The field of television production

This section turns to the empirical study of the Swedish field of television production. The aim is to illustrate the main steps in field analysis while at the same time revealing the structures of a contemporary field of cultural production. It follows Bourdieu's (2000) three steps of field analysis and starts with (1) a sketch on the genesis of the field, turning then to (2) the contemporary structure of the field, and finally (3) agents' position-takings within the field.

Genesis

In *The Rules of Art*, Bourdieu (1996) analyzes the genesis of the literary field in order to trace the origins of its contemporary structure. Bourdieu primarily focuses on the 1848 revolution and how key social agents were able to carve out new positions in the field. Fligstein and McAdam (2012: 91), on the other hand, stress that there are "four dynamics that typically shape the process of field formation": (1) state facilitation, (2) mobilization of social actors with a common goal, (3) the settlement of the field's order by key social actors, and (4) the formation of internal governance units securing the reproduction of the field. Indeed, in modern history, the state has been a "major catalyst" in the formation of fields, not least because of its stakes in dealing with, and taking advantage of, technological advancements (Fligstein & McAdam, 2012: 88). Electronic mass communication was one such innovation that many states monopolized at the outset. This was the case for television in Sweden in the 1950s. Like the UK tradition of broadcasting in the name of "public service", the purpose of broadcasting was to inform, educate, and entertain the public (Reith, 1924). The state provided the broadcasting infrastructure, concession rights, license agreements, and funding, and created the organizational vehicle (based on its forerunner Swedish Radio) that would harbor television production until the 1980s: Sveriges Television (SVT). This implied that it was the state and the political field that consecrated the first incumbents in the field of television production and mobilized actors with a common goal (Fligstein & McAdam, 2012).

Despite being subjected to the logics of the political field, the public service organization made independence from the state and other organized interests one of its main pillars. There are thus grounds for speaking about a burgeoning autonomy within television production already in the 1950s, not least due to professionalization and the import of journalistic values. The existence of shared understandings among players in the field, a doxa, and the emergence of specific capital in the field is supported by the fact that the term "TV-artsmanship" (Engblom, 1998) gradually came to be used amongst agents in the field.

In the 1980s, the field was invaded "by outside groups" (Fligstein & McAdam, 2012: 99). A political majority adhered to commercial actors lobbying for deregulation of the media market and SVT faced competition from commercial companies. This constitutes an example of how fields change due to "exogenous shocks" such as changes in neighboring fields (the political field) (Fligstein & McAdam, 2012). At the same time, however, the new hybrid channel TV4, and independent production companies, adopted much of the public service ethos from SVT (Graffman, 2002; Bolin, 2004). With Bourdieu (1996) we must thus stress that transformations of fields are negotiated within the existing positions in the field, and that the commercial position emerged from a field permeated by a public service vision on broadcasting.

In its emerging phase, the main "internal governance units" (Fligstein & McAdam, 2012) securing reproduction and stability were government authorities (at present, the Swedish Media Agency). The 1990s witnessed the rise and increased popularity of educational programs oriented toward media production (including the institutionalization of media and communication studies at Swedish universities). As a consequence of the field gradually maturing and gaining autonomy, field-internal juries granting awards for television production were formed: *Kristallen* (2005) and *Ria* (2011). In 2009, the organization Swedish Film & TV Producers Association was founded, with separate sections for the production of film, television, and commercials.

Social fields tend to be hierarchized between incumbents (Fligstein & McAdam, 2012) or consecrated agents (Bourdieu, 1996) on the one hand, and newcomers and non-consecrated avantgarde on the other. From this brief sketch of the genesis of the Swedish field of television production we also learn about the historical tension between public and commercial broadcasting, which in some respects echoes the oppositions between autonomous production and heteronomous production outlined by Bourdieu (1996). Heteronomy in this field is, however, multifaceted and applies in different ways to public and commercial producers, as indicated in the previous section. We furthermore learn that from relatively early on, field-specific capital emerged (the public service ethos and "TV-artsmanship"), and internal governance units are in place to secure stability and reproduction in the field by consecrating agents (by awarding prizes) and by calling out those who fail to abide by its rules (the Swedish Media Authority).

While globalization and digitization affect television production on both a market and an organizational level (Straubhaar, 2007), the field still retains a national character that is upheld by the inclination to produce domestic television (Kuipers, 2015). There is, however, no doubt that domestic production, primarily in commercial broadcasting, is challenged by the economic backlash (recent examples in Sweden include Viaplay's downscaling and an uncertain future for TV4). This might imply that the national field of television production will primarily be upheld by public service institutions (which nonetheless face both political and economic pressures) and that commercial production becomes increasingly subsumed by an international field of cultural production. Additionally, various content creators, such as YouTube influencers in "online fields" that primarily abide by platform-based attention economies (Levina & Arriaga, 2014), have also increased their presence in the televisual landscape. Although the contents produced by these actors are part and parcel of many people's media repertoires, the question regarding the extent to which they are affected by the effects in the field of television production can be debated. Since these agents do not normally share the stakes (illusio) and norms (doxa) that bind agents to the field of television production, they have not been included in the present analyses.

Structure of the field

To study the contemporary structure of the field of television production and position-takings within the field, MCA was applied to a survey deployed in 2019 (before the current economic crisis in domestic television production) including 378 agents in the field (including journalists, editors, hosts, technicians, assistants, managers, owners, interns, writers, directors, producers, casters, etc.).

Box 5.2 The field of television production: active variables

Eleven active variables were used to construct a statistical representation of the Swedish field of television production, and as such the present analysis follows the social space/field approach delineated in

Chapter 3. Both seniority in the field and having received an award, or having the power to consecrate others by granting awards, have been shown to be important field-specific capitals in other fields of cultural production (Bourdieu, 1996; Hovden, 2008; Duval, 2016). Accordingly, the MCA was based on (1) years in television production and (2) having won a prize for television production/having been a member of a jury granting awards. In Swedish broadcasting, public service is endowed with particular value, and being affiliated with these institutions may practically function as capital in the field (Graffman, 2002; Bolin, 2004). The analysis thus includes (3) working in public service broadcasting or in a commercial production company. A fourth variable, (4) genre of television production, captures whether an agent produces collectively recognized genres of journalism and film/drama or less prestigious and "new" genres such as Reality-TV. Finally, (5) influence on the production process was used to measure the degree of power and influence at the workplace.

Bourdieu's (1996) analysis of Gustave Flaubert, Charles Baudelaire, Léon Cladel, Marcel Duchamp, and other agents in the field of cultural production stresses that players in a particular field are simultaneously agents in the wider space of class relations (social space). Agents are thus endowed with different amounts of economic, cultural, and social capital. The choice of these variables was based on the previous studies of the Swedish social space (Lindell, 2018) similar to the analysis in Chapter 3. Cultural capital was measured with (6) level of education, and cultural inheritance in terms of (7) if respondents' parents have/had university degrees, and if they had (8) grown up in a culturally rich home. Economic capital was measured by (9) income and (10) owning a country house/summer residence. Lastly, social capital was measured by (11) board membership.

Figure 5.1 represents the structure of distribution of capitals in the field.[1] The first two axes, which are analyzed here, explain 73 percent of the inertia in the eleven active variables. As in virtually all social fields (Fligstein & McAdam, 2012), one (the horizontal) axis (43.1 percent) separates the dominant from the dominated agents. The axis describes the opposition between the consecrated establishment and non-consecrated or new agents. Agents in the right side of the space have both more seniority in broadcasting and more influence over the production process, and they are more likely to have received an award/been a member of a jury granting awards. They have, in short, power over both television production and consecration in the field. Additionally, they have high economic capital (high salaries and summer residences) and social capital (board membership). By contrast, the left-hand side

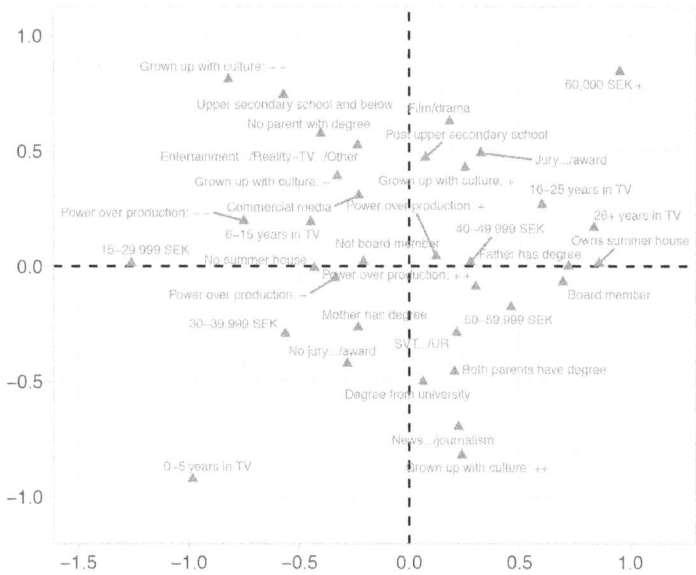

Figure 5.1 The Swedish field of television production. Cloud of categories

of the space gathers less experienced and non-consecrated players with less economic and social capital.

The vertical axis (30 percent) primarily separates different volumes of cultural capital and types of broadcasting (genre and organization). Agents located at the bottom of the space have higher amounts of cultural capital: they tend to be well-educated cultural inheritors (having been raised by parents with academic degrees within homes rich in cultural artifacts and expressions). The opposite goes for those at the top who have lower amounts of cultural capital but more economic capital (in the top right). Although different regions in the Swedish field of television production are autonomous from different external forces (e.g., public service media is autonomous from the market but dependent on the political field for funding and license agreements), this axis reveals some traces of the autonomy/heteronomy opposition described by Bourdieu (1996). The bottom of the space is characterized by an overrepresentation of agents in the field's legacy media: the public service sector and the news and journalism genres. Both journalists and public service producers are, or explicitly seek to be, autonomous from various external interests. In fact, 98 percent of the producers surveyed legitimize public service by agreeing to the statement that SVT produces "quality TV", which speaks to the notion that the most autonomous regions in the field tend also to have amassed internal recognition. In the upper half of the space, we find commercial producers as well as the production of fiction and/or entertainment (such as Reality-TV).

The structure of the Swedish field of television production resembles the general structure of the fields of cultural production proposed by Bourdieu (1996). The field is doubly hierarchized. First, according to seniority and workplace power, where the established and well-paid producers endowed with the power of consecration stand against (young) challengers and newcomers, and second according to volumes of cultural capital and certain field-specific capital, where "pure" and more autonomous production geared toward educating and informing audiences, produced by agents rich in cultural capital, stands in contrast to both commercial logics of the media industry and film/drama producers. In line with previous discussions we note, however, that the notion of autonomy, in particular its assumed correlation with small-scale production, is not straightforward in the field of television production.

Position-takings within the field

Figure 5.2 studies a range of position-takings as supplementary variables. Along the horizontal axis, we observe that dominant positions in the field correspond with a taste for institutionalized culture (classical concerts) and the framing of one's job in broadcasting as an intellectual undertaking. Dominated positions instead foster the opposite attitudes and lifestyles and, interestingly, the tendency to construct governmental authorities as legitimate judges on what constitutes "quality television". Along the vertical axis, we identify the recognition (in the commercial/entertainment pole) or rejection (in the cultural capital /journalism pole) of commercial television channels and production companies. Established producers in public service television and journalism, where cultural capital outweighs economic capital in agents' capital compositions (bottom right), are more inclined to describe their job as an intellectual undertaking. Unlike agents in the dominated and more commercial region of the space, they are also frequent book readers and consumers of the institutionalized culture (classical concerts and museums). Like their counterparts in the wider social space (explored in Chapter 4), agents in the bottom right region tend to reject commercial channels and the affiliated production companies. Furthermore, the elites in this field share the taste for the institutionalized culture with the dominant regions of the wider social space. This gives some support to the existence of a homologous relationship between the fields of cultural consumption and production (Bourdieu, 1996). By contrast, established producers in the commercial and entertainment-oriented sector of the field, where economic capital outweighs cultural capital (top right), value the quality of the commercial production companies Anagram (with a film and drama profile) and ELK (which produces a mixture of game shows, factual entertainment, and Reality-TV).

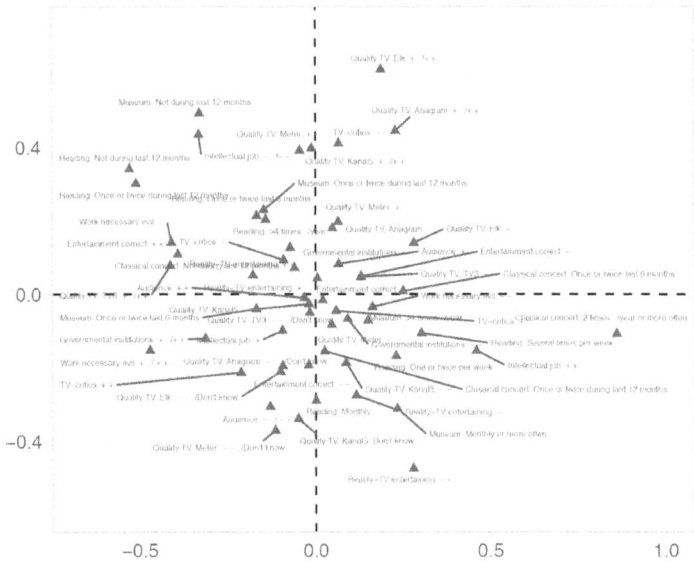

Figure 5.2 Position-takings within the Swedish field of television production. Cloud of categories

The tendency to legitimize the position of television critics as taste keepers decreases as we move from the non-consecrated regions of the more "autonomous" pole to the regions dedicated foremost to commercial production. Agents in commercial production tend to instead value the judgments of television audiences.

The study of the distribution of various position-takings (including views on the profession, quality TV, relationships to other stakeholders, and broader lifestyles) gives the indication that the structure of the field is corroborated by the position-takings assumed by agents in the different regions of the field. In other words, the objective positions (Figure 5.1) in the field constitute vantage points from where agents position themselves and, in effect, reproduce the structure of the field. Importantly, it is from positions in the field of television production that its agents operate as cultural intermediaries and tastemakers (Bourdieu, 1984) and grant voice and visibility to actors in other fields, and by that token exercise their "meta-capital" (Couldry, 2003). Put differently, field analysis provides insights into the positions from which agents in these fields exercise their "power of consecration – the power to say who and what is important, and what we should think about important things and people" (Champagne, 2005: 58). In this sense, we note that, elites in the field of television production are elites in the broader social space as well (high salaries and cultural capital). We also note that the taste-making elites and decision-makers in broadcasting are drawn to the institutionalized and legitimized culture, whereas precarious work in Reality-TV productions correspond to a lack of scholastic capital and overall lack of (fine) cultural participation. By teasing out the structures and position-takings within fields of media production, field analysis provides important insights that supplement traditional approaches in our discipline, including ethnographies of particular organizational cultures, macro-level political-economic analyses of media markets, and in-depth textual analyses of media representations.

Exploring the structure of an academic field

MCA is usually based on survey data, like in the studies of the social space and media practices (Chapter 4) and the field of television production in this chapter. In MCA research, however, it is perfectly possible to use data gathered from archives, magazines, biographies, databases, online repositories, and other sources. In many ways this kind of data can be more reliable than the self-reported data provided by surveys. In historical research on fields, it is, of course, necessary to turn to archives of various kinds. Bourdieusian prosopography involves gathering and systematizing existing data to study a "collective biography" (Broady, 2002: 381). In Broady's (2002: 381–382) definition, prosopography involves (1) studying individuals in the same field, (2) collecting comprehensive data on players in the given field, particularly in terms of their field-specific capital, (3) gathering the same data on all individuals, and (4) focusing on the field as such rather than on individuals. These points put emphasis on the use of MCA as a method of analysis. Prosopography has been used in the historical and longitudinal study of social fields, such as the literary field (Sapiro, 2002) and not least the academic field (Bourdieu, 1988).

This section relies on prosopographic data on all agents active in the Swedish field of media and communication studies in 2020. It studies the agents in this field (N = 254) as found in public registers: research biographies/presentations on university websites, publications and metrics in Diva and Libris (national archives/libraries) and Google Scholar, and annual reports from the biggest national research funders. Focus is put on the distribution of a range of field-specific capitals (e.g., seniority, number of publications, external funding) and onto-epistemological positions (sub-fields, theoretical approaches to communication) in the field. Using such prosopographic data in MCA allows teasing out the basic structures of the field.

Bourdieu approaches academia as a field: "even the 'purest' science is a social field like any other, with its distribution of power and its monopolies, its struggles and strategies, interests and profits" (Bourdieu, 1975: 19). It can easily be argued that Swedish media and communication studies constitute a field in its own right, as it gathers agents that have in common the investment (illusio) in understanding and explaining media and communication. Like other fields, the emergence of this field was sanctioned by the state following a growing concern with "media society" and the challenges it evoked (Hyvönen et al., 2018). The field is relatively autonomous and abides by its own logic of practice, which manifests in its focus (e.g., study object), discipline-specific university degrees, journals, conferences, and theoretical concepts. This also implies that various "internal governance units" that consecrate agents are in place (Fligstein & McAdam, 2012). These include the educational programs that award the PhD, which have been in existence since the 1990s, and a nation-wide organization granting awards (The Association for Swedish Media and Communication Research) as well as national training programs for PhD students.

Figure 5.3 is a statistical representation of the structure of the field.[2] The horizontal axis accounts for 62 percent of the variation among the variables. Having received a research grant from the Swedish Research Council and the number of publications/citations are the most important active variables in this dimension. The axis opposes consecrated agents (holding a PhD) with PhD students; recipients of research grants stand against those without external funding; and the publication elite stands against those who have published less or nothing. The horizontal dimension describes, in other words, a hierarchy separating an incumbency (right) from challengers and newcomers (left), and the volumes of field-specific capital (in academic/cultural, symbolic, and economic forms). As argued above, this kind of differentiation is identified in most fields (Fligstein & McAdam, 2012).

The vertical axis explains 10 percent of the variation and can be understood as a contemporary variant of what has been described as the historical "tug-of-war" between behavioral/psychologically oriented research (e.g., on various forms of media effects) and more "critical" and humanistic perspectives (Hyvönen et al., 2018: 93). This axis thus taps into the historical divisions between critical and administrative research (Lazarsfeld, 1941), as it separates agents and institutions on the basis of differences in theoretical approaches and investments in various sub-fields. The social distances between the sub-fields of political communication and strategic and organization communication (top) and (post-)Marxist domains of semiotics, cultural studies, and critical theory (bottom) are notable. In some respects, these symbolic divisions are reflected in physical space, since agents in the respective regions tend to gather at different institutions, attend different conferences, and publish in altogether different outlets.

We could argue that the horizontal axis deals with *time* – a requirement for gaining high positions in the field, as well as a resource controlled by agents endowed with the social resources and authority required to "influence the way in which [other] agents allocate their time" (Bourdieu, 1988:

Subfield: Political communication

Subfield: Strategic.../org. communication

Sociopsychological

Old universities

Has PhD

Monographs: >4

VR_Grant_No

Google H-index: >11

Monographs: 0

Journal articles: 11-20

Journal articles: >21

PhD Student

VR_Grant_Yes

Journal articles: 0

Critical

Subfield: Cultural studies

RJ_Grant_Yes

University colleges

Semiotic

Monographs: 3

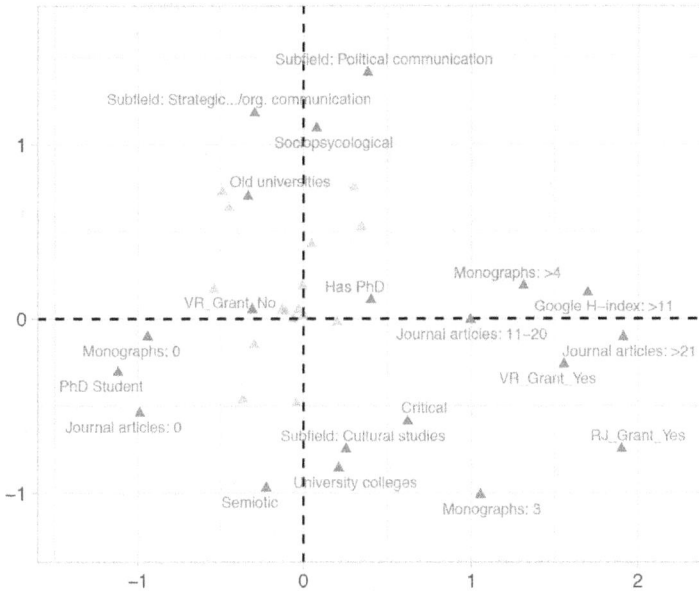

Figure 5.3 The Swedish field of media and communication studies. Cloud of categories

98). By contrast, the vertical axis taps into the different mental and physical *spaces* occupied by agents in the field: it captures differences in how to best understand and study media and communication. The structure of the field resembles the structures of other fields of cultural production (including the field of television production), wherein agents are divided in terms of their volumes of field-specific capital or level of consecration, and in terms of their ideologies of practice (Bourdieu, 1975; Sapiro, 2002; Hovden, 2008; Duval, 2016). Both of these structures affect the position-takings of agents in the field, including the "rules" pertaining to everyday social interaction between senior and junior staff, styles of writing, preferred journals and conferences, and not least the views on how to best understand and explain media and communication. This raises questions regarding the field-specific positions from which researchers explain the world, and how to overcome divisions and hierarchies in academia.

Conclusion

The notion of field presents a relatively unique unit of analysis to media scholars (Benson & Neveu, 2005). Located at the mezzo-level, the concept forces a media researcher to look "below" the levels of media systems, policy regimes, journalistic cultures, and capitalism and the "attention economy" at large. It also prompts us to look "above" the individual strategies of content creators, journalists, television producers, and the intricacies of specific media texts. Field analysis allows us, in other words, to study the participants inside relatively autonomous social microcosms that revolve around specific struggles and require certain investments. Applying field analysis in media and communication studies implies shedding light on a range of microcosms that constitute sub-fields in the broader field of cultural production. While television production, the arts, journalism, and academia differ on many counts, they share the power to represent the social world (through publication, news broadcasts, television shows) (Couldry, 2003; Bourdieu, 2005). They constitute fields of production whose products are evaluated and incorporated in a corresponding field of consumption (the social space). As such, field analysis as applied to the study of media and cultural production does not only reveal something broadly about how human beings organize themselves into hierarchical social structures, and how these structures become reproduced in position-takings. It also discloses how such hierarchies form the positions from which agents in these fields exercise their symbolic power, that is, their power to construct the social world (Bourdieu, 1991).

This chapter has illustrated how the study of fields can be conducted with MCA – a method that allows unearthing the "hidden structures" of fields (Duval, 2018: 519). As discussed in Chapter 3, MCA-oriented field analysis can be supplemented with qualitative methods (e.g., interviews) in order to close in on agents' subjective position-takings that emerge at the objective positions in the field. Digital methods may also supplement field analysis, and this will be the topic in the next chapter.

Notes

1 The ten active categories that contribute most to axis 1 (Figure 5.1) are (in hierarchical order): "Owns summer house", "0–5 years in television", "15–29,999 SEK/month", "16–25 years in television", "No summer house", "60,000 SEK+/month", "Board membership", "26+ years in television", "30–39,999 SEK/month", and "Grown up with culture: – –". For axis 2 these are: "Grown up with culture: + +", "News/journalism", "0–5 years in television", "Entertainment/Reality TV/Other", "Degree from university", "No parent with degree", "Jury/award", "No jury/award", "60,000 SEK+/month", and "Post upper secondary school".

2 The ten active categories that contribute most to axis 1 (Figure 5.3) are (in hierarchical order): "VR grant: yes", "H–index: >11", "PhD Student", "Journal articles: >20", "Monographs: 0", "Journal articles: 0", "RJ grant: yes", "Monographs: >4", "Journal articles: 11–20", and "Has PhD". For axis 3 these are "Trad: Socio-psychological", "Sub: Strat./Org. Comm.", "University college", "Sub: Pol. Comm.", "Sub: Cultural Studies", "Old university", "Journal articles: 0", "Sub: Journalism Studies", "Monographs: 0", and H–index: 6–10". Note that figure 5.3 focuses on axis 1 and 3: the second axis taps into the first as it describes an opposition between consecrated and non-consecrated agents.

References

Benson, R., & Neveu, E. (Eds.). (2005). *Bourdieu and the journalistic field*. Cambridge: Polity.

Bolin, G. (2004). The value of being public service: The shifting of power relations in Swedish television production. *Media, Culture & Society, 26*(2), 277–287.

Bolin, G. (2009). Symbolic production and value in media industries. *Journal of Cultural Economy, 2*(3), 345–361.

Bolin, G. (2012). The forms of value: Problems of convertibility in field theory. *tripleC: Communication, Capitalism & Critique. Open Access Journal for a Global Sustainable Information Society, 10*(1), 33–41.

Bourdieu, P. (1975). The specificity of the scientific field and the social conditions of the progress of reason. *Information (International Social Science Council), 14*(6), 19–47.

Bourdieu, P. (1984). *Distinction: A social critique of the judgement of taste*. New York: Routledge.

Bourdieu, P. (1988). *Homo academicus*. Stanford, CA: Stanford University Press.

Bourdieu, P. (1991). *Language and symbolic power*. Cambridge: Polity.

Bourdieu, P. (1996). *The rules of art: Genesis and structure of the literary field*. Cambridge: Polity.

Bourdieu, P. (1998). *On television and journalism*. London: Pluto Press.

Bourdieu, P. (2000). *Konstens regler: Det litterära fältets uppkomst och struktur* [The rules of art: Genesis and structure of the literary field]. Stockholm: Brutus Östlings Bokförlag.

Bourdieu, P. (2005). The political field, the social field, and the journalistic field. In R. Benson & E. Neveu (Eds.), *Bourdieu and the journalistic field* (pp. 29–47). Cambridge: Polity.

Bourdieu, P., & Wacquant, L. (1992). *An invitation to reflexive sociology*. Cambridge: Polity.

Broady, D. (2002). French prosopography: definition and suggested readings. *Poetics, 30*(5–6), 381–385.

Buchholz, L. (2016). What is a global field? Theorizing fields beyond the nation-state. *The Sociological Review, 64*(2_suppl), 31–60.

Champagne, P. (2005). The "double dependency": The journalistic field between politics and markets. In R. Benson & E. Neveu (Eds.), *Bourdieu and the journalistic field* (pp. 48–63). Cambridge: Polity.

Couldry, N. (2003). Media meta-capital: Extending the range of Bourdieu's field theory. *Theory and Society, 32*, 653–677.

Duval, J. (2005). Economic journalism in France. In R. Benson & E. Neveu (Eds), *Bourdieu and the journalistic field* (pp. 135–155). Cambridge: Polity.

Duval, J. (2016). *Le Cinéma au XXe siècle. Entre loi du marché et règles de l'art*. Paris: CNRS editions.

Duval, J. (2018). Correspondence analysis and Bourdieu's use of statistics: Using correspondence analysis within field theory. In T. Medvetz & J. J. Sallaz (Eds.), *The Oxford handbook of Pierre Bourdieu* (pp. 512–527). Oxford: Oxford University Press.

Engblom, L. Å. (1998). *Radio- och TV-folket: rekryteringen av programmedarbetare till radion och televisionen i Sverige 1925–1995* [The radio and television people: The recruitment of hosts to radio and television in Sweden 1925–1995]. Stockholm: Rabén Prisma.

Fligstein, N., & McAdam, D. (2012). *A theory of fields*. Oxford: Oxford University Press.

Graffman, K. (2002). *Kommersiell mediekultur: En etnografisk studie av TV-producenter och TV-produktion* [Commercial media culture: An ethnographic study of TV-producers and TV-production]. [Doctoral dissertation, Uppsala University. Acta Universitatis Upsaliensis].

Hallin, D. C., & Mancini, P. (2004). *Comparing media systems: Three models of media and politics*. Cambridge: Cambridge University Press.

Hesmondhalgh, D. (2006). Bourdieu, the media and cultural production. *Media, Culture & Society, 28*(2), 211–231.

Hjarvard, S. (2008). The mediatization of society: A theory of the media as agents of social and cultural change. *Nordicom Review, 29*(2), 105–134.

Hovden, J. F. (2008). *Profane and sacred. A Study of the Norwegian journalistic field*. Bergen: University of Bergen.

Hyvönen, M., Snickars, P., & Vesterlund, P. (2018). The formation of Swedish media studies, 1960–1980. *Media History, 24*(1), 86–98.

Kuipers, G. (2015). How national institutions mediate the global: Screen translation, institutional interdependencies, and the production of national difference in four European countries. *American Sociological Review, 80*(5), 985–1013.

Lazarsfeld, P. F. (1941). Remarks on administrative and critical communications research. *Zeitschrift für Sozialforschung, 9*(1), 2–16.

Levina, N., & Arriaga, M. (2014). Distinction and status production on user-generated content platforms: Using Bourdieu's theory of cultural production to understand social dynamics in online fields. *Information Systems Research, 25*(3), 468–488.

Lindblom, T., Lindell, J., & Gidlund, K. (2022). Digitalizing the journalistic field: Journalists' views on changes in journalistic autonomy, capital and habitus. *Digital Journalism*, 1–20.

Lindell, J. (2015). Bourdieusian media studies: Returning social theory to old and new media. *Distinktion: Scandinavian Journal of Social Theory, 16*(3), 362–377.

Lindell, J. (2018). *Distinction* recapped: Digital news repertoires in the class structure. *New Media & Society, 20*(8), 3029–3049.

Lundahl, O. (2022). Algorithmic meta-capital: Bourdieusian analysis of social power through algorithms in media consumption. *Information, Communication & Society, 25*(10), 1440–1455.

Maares, P., & Hanusch, F. (2022). Interpretations of the journalistic field: A systematic analysis of how journalism scholarship appropriates Bourdieusian thought. *Journalism, 23*(4), 736–754.

Marantz, E. A., & Cattani, G. (2024). Changing of the guards: Status dynamics and innovation in American TV shows, 1956–2010. *Poetics, 102*, 101859.

Mears, A. (2023). Bringing Bourdieu to a content farm: Social media production fields and the cultural economy of attention. *Social Media + Society*, e-pub ahead of print.

Reith, J. C. W. (1924). *Broadcast over Britain*. London: Hodder and Stoughton limited.

Sapiro, G. (2002). The structure of the French literary field during the German occupation (1940–1944): A multiple correspondence analysis. *Poetics, 30*(5–6), 387–402.

Sapiro, G. (2018). Field theory from a transnational perspective. In T. Medvetz & J. J. Sallaz (Eds.), *The Oxford handbook of Pierre Bourdieu* (pp. 161–182). Oxford: Oxford University Press.

Slaatta, T. (2016). Micro vs. macro: A reflection on the potentials of field analysis. In C. Paterson, D. Lee, A. Saha, & A. Zoellner (Eds.), *Advancing media production research: Shifting sites, methods, and politics* (pp. 95–111). London: Palgrave Macmillan UK.

Solaroli, M. (2016). The rules of a middle-brow art: Digital production and cultural consecration in the global field of professional photojournalism. *Poetics, 59*, 50–66.

Straubhaar, J. D. (2007). *World television: From global to local.* Thousand Oaks, CA: Sage.

Willig, I. (2016). Field theory and media production: A bridge-building strategy. In C. Paterson, D. Lee, A. Saha, & A. Zoellner (Eds.), *Advancing media production research* (pp. 53–67). London: Palgrave Macmillan.

6   Digital Bourdieu

Introduction

Field theory can be used to shed light on key dynamics of the digital media landscape. A central point that has been repeated throughout this book, and that on numerous occasions has been pointed out by Bourdieu himself (e.g., Bourdieu, 1991a), is that field theory is not tied to the (analogue) empirical conditions under which it was fashioned. The two previous chapters studied social inequality in relation to the uses of digital media and raised questions regarding changing dynamics in social fields following technological innovations in media production. Ignatow and Robinson (2017) stress that field theory has flourished in various strands of digital sociology precisely because it was designed to be put to use in different empirical settings in open-ended ways.

In current digital sociology it is possible to identify two main approaches to putting Bourdieu to use in the analysis of digital media (Romele & Rodighiero, 2020). On the one hand, we can, as I have done in Chapters 4 and 5, apply field theory in the contemporary digital setting in order to answer research questions that resonate with Bourdieu's original aims. This includes the study of how digitalization might transform structures of fields, for example in how smartphones and amateur photography can push professional photojournalism closer to the art field (Solaroli, 2016), and inquiries into correspondences between (digitalized) lifestyles and social positions (Lindell, 2018). On the other hand, we can place "Bourdieu inside the digital", and use elements of field theory to theorize the digital in itself (Romele & Rodighiero, 2020: 99). Works in this strand include conceptualizing data as capital (Sadowski, 2019) and efforts to theorize technology and digital media as "crystalized habitus" (Sterne, 2003), "digital habitus" (Romele & Rodighiero, 2020), or "machine habitus" (Airoldi, 2022). This "inside" view constitutes a theoretical intervention in the discussions on algorithmic culture, agency, and technology. It is argued that digital machines and algorithm-driven platforms are *"habitus* producers and reproducers" (Romele & Rodighiero, 2020: 99, italics in original) because algorithmic curation "makes you desire only what /.../ you

DOI: 10.4324/9781003364245-6

can, according to your status, have access to" (Romele & Rodighiero, 2020: 110–111; see also Gaw, 2022; Lundahl, 2022).

In this chapter I present a Bourdieusian approach to a main method used in making sense of and visualizing patterns of interaction on digital platforms – social network analysis (SNA). The argument is that while Bourdieu remained skeptical of network analysis, this method, when applied to large patterns within "found data" (Bruhn Jensen, 2010) scraped from digital platforms, can supplement the analysis of social fields in important ways. In a sense, then, this chapter is located between the two perspectives on how to put Bourdieu to use in relation to "the digital". The approach presented here, which amounts to scraping interactions from a social networking site and analyzing transactions of recognition, can be said to remain "outside" the digital because it treats the analysis of digital interactions as supplementary to multiple correspondence analysis (MCA). The aim is not to theorize "the digital" in itself, but to add new tools to field theory and answer questions regarding the character of social fields. The approach is nonetheless "inside" the digital because empirical focus is put on digital units of analysis novel to the Bourdieusian approach (as outlined in Chapter 3). The next section spells out the Bourdieusian approach to SNA and what role this method can play in Bourdieusian media studies. The following sections theorize interaction on digital platforms in terms of field theory and present the empirical study of the Swedish field of cultural production.

Studying fields in a datafied world

The digital revolution and the internet implied that data is generated and collected at an unprecedent rate: "More data were accumulated in 2002 than all previous years of human history combined" (Bail, 2014: 465). The ability to collect data on and analyze human behavior in the era of datafication, where more and more aspects of social life become quantified, not least by our activity on social networking sites, brings about "new and opaque regimes of population management, control, discrimination and exclusion" (Kennedy et al., 2015: 1). For good reasons, critical scholars have highlighted the threats of increasing surveillance, or "dataveillance" (Kennedy et al., 2015: 1), "surveillance capitalism" (Zuboff, 2015), and "data colonialism" – the combination of "predatory extractive practices of historical colonialism with the abstract quantification methods of computing" (Couldry & Mejias, 2019: 337). Significant parts of critical scholarship on "big data" thus revolve around its detrimental effects on social life.

There exists, however, a parallel debate among social scientists, since the datafication of social relations implies that researchers have "big data" at their disposal (Burrows & Savage, 2014). Big data is, to paraphrase Kitchin (2014: 1–2), huge in volume, high in velocity, diverse in variety, exhaustive in scope, fine-grained in resolution, relational in nature, and flexible. As such it offers ample opportunities to "measure culture" (Mohr et al., 2020). However, despite the many potentials of big data analysis, cultural sociology has lagged behind when it comes to incorporating it into its methodological arsenal (Bail, 2014). Some commentators even hold that tech-savvy actors outside academia now "produce better sociology than … sociologists themselves" (Osborne et al. in Burrows & Savage, 2014: 3). For Bail (2014), however, social scientists possess the theoretical resources needed in order to make use of big data in ways that can enrich understandings of social and cultural life. By adopting big data analysis, we can approach our objects of study and research questions in ways that were unthinkable not long ago (Bail, 2014). A key example for Bail is the notion of discursive fields (which includes Bourdieu's field concept). This concept makes ecological claims about vast social systems (the literary field, the social space, academia, the journalistic field, etc.) that are difficult, if not impossible, to study in their entirety with surveys and other methods that are based on "accounts of actions" in (more or less) representative samples (Burrows & Savage, 2014: 3). Yet this is exactly how sociologists have gone about studying fields. In Bail's view, then, we have up until recently been unable to observe "meso- or macro-level relationships between social actors and cultural elements that most scholars believe create such social spaces" (2014: 469). Indeed, fields are "so broad that an entire team of researchers working for several years could only map a fraction of all the texts, transcripts, or archives that define them" (Bail, 2014: 469). This would explain why "cultural sociologists have scarcely theorized the outer limits of cultural fields, the spaces between them, or the relationships among multiple fields" (Bail, 2014: 469). This chapter begins to unpack how such questions can be approached with SNA.

Data scraped off of digital platforms captures action "naturally occurring" (Bail, 2014: 467), contrasting surveys and interviews that produce accounts of actions in data "made" by a researcher (Bruhn Jensen, 2010). Additionally, in big data analysis the n-count equals "all" (Kitchin, 2014), meaning that (in the best-case scenario) problems of skewed survey data and the issues this brings to inferential statistics can be circumvented. This offers new ways of collecting (e.g., automated scraping) and analyzing data that allow mapping the contours of discursive fields (Bail, 2014). As shown in Chapter 3, in Bourdieusian sociology the endeavor to establish the existence of a social field demands a meticulous ethnographic understanding of the social dynamics that tie social agents to a specific common sense and logic of practice (doxa), their investments in the stakes of the game (illusio), and the resources that are collectively recognized (field-specific capital). The limits of a field, located at the point where the field has no effect (Bourdieu, 2000: 327–328), are even more difficult to ascertain in the study of a sample of respondents. How, indeed, can one know if one has reached the outer boundary of a field by studying respondents that have been sampled on the premise that they are players in the field? If, on the other hand, we are able to collect and analyze all interactions revolving around a specific issue or entity central to a given field, we would be able to get an initial grip on the field's scope. It goes without saying that the ability to identify the (transactional) traces of social fields and their outer limits could move Bourdieusian research forward in productive ways.

Network theory and analysis originate in Durkheim's writings (Segre, 2004) and in other classical sociology, such as Tönnies and Simmel (Scott, 2012). It was further developed in the 20th century and has relatively recently come to see an increased popularity due to the networked architecture of the internet, and because of its ability to make sense of big data (Otte & Rousseau, 2002; Elgendy & Elragal, 2014; Mohr et al., 2020). SNA maps complex social relations by focusing on nodes (e.g., persons, organizations, social media accounts) and the edges between them (relationships and interactions such as "likes") (Otte & Rousseau, 2002). Unlike surveys, network analysis is applied to relational data rather than variable or attribute data, as it "focuses on the characteristics of ties rather than on the characteristics of the individual members" (Wetherell et al. in Otte & Rosseau, 2002: 442).

Despite its obvious focus on relations rather than substances, which is a key focus in field theory (see Chapter 3), Bourdieu rejected network analysis. For him, this method focuses on the wrong kind of relationality, that is, on more or less ephemeral *reflections* of social structures such as communication patterns, interactions, and other relationships between agents. In field theory, the researcher's task is to map the structure of the distribution of objective forms of domination – the possession of capital – and how these form the social conditions from which various position-takings and practices emerge (see Chapter 3). Bourdieu looks for relations between *positions* rather than relations between agents (Bottero & Crossley, 2011: 114). It follows that in network analysis, the study of broad and robust social structures "has been sacrificed to the analysis of the particular linkages" (Bourdieu & Wacquant, 1992: 114). This kind of critique of "nodocentrism", which is argued to put forward an "incomplete picture" of social relations, has echoed in discussions on SNA (and the modeling of the social world it promotes when being applied in the design of online platforms) (Mejias, 2010: 612).

These differences and tensions notwithstanding, scholars have convincingly shown that SNA rhymes well with Bourdieu's relational approach to the social world. In his "manifesto for a relational sociology", Emirbayer (1997) echoes Bourdieu's distinction between relational and substantialist approaches (see Chapter 3), arguing that SNA facilitates the study of transactions (rather than fixed substances) that lie at the core of social life. Others have empirically proved that SNA can be used alongside MCA to uncover structures of social fields (Anheier et al., 1995). For instance, De Nooy (2003) showed similarities in the outputs from SNA and MCA applied to the same data, and Sivertsen (2023) combines Meta's "Audience insights" data tracing Facebook users' preferences with MCA to uncover the social stratification of cultural practices. Some network analysts, however, have castigated Bourdieu for providing "an insufficiently worked-out conception of social ties and the networks they form" (Bottero & Crossley, 2011: 100; see also Mohr, 2013). According to them, it is SNA rather than MCA that offers the tools necessary to account for the mechanisms described by field theory:

> From where and by what means, for example, do occupants of a given region of social space acquire the taste for certain forms of music if not from one another in *relations* of mutual influence? /.../ actors who are proximate in social space have (more) similar habitus because they are more likely to be *interacting* with one another, mutually influencing one another and therefore mutually shaping their respective habitus.
>
> (Bottero & Crossley, 2011: 101–102, italics added)

Evidently, field theory and MCA tend to downplay interaction and relationships, as these are approached as "consequences rather than the sources and causes of social structure" (De Nooy, 2003: 317).

On the one hand, I agree with Bourdieu's (Bourdieu & Wacquant, 1992: 114) argument that structures of interaction uncovered by SNA should be viewed not as representations of the field-as-such, but rather as traces of the field-in-action. Interactions are not the same as social structures (De Nooy, 2003). On the other hand, in following De Nooy (2003), Bail (2014), and Singh (2016), I hold that there is value in using SNA on digital data that entails all interactions surrounding a specific node, which in effect captures action *in situ* rather than the accounts of action that respondents of a survey provide. If interactions and relations between agents reveal how a field is performed, it follows that SNA allows mapping social fields and their contours: "if field relations *manifest* themselves in networks, as he [Bourdieu] suggests, then such interconnections can *identify* field relations" (Bottero & Crossley, 2011: 101, italics in original). SNA promotes a focus on practice (De Nooy, 2003: 322), which should lie close to heart for Bourdieusian scholars, particularly as a supplement to the study of relations between objective positions promoted by MCA. While SNA does not study "structures" in the Bourdieusian sense of mapping agents' access to forms of capital (De Nooy, 2003), it can, for instance, map the patterns of recognition that reveal which "players" are considered "worthy" by other players in the field. This approach is in line with the assumption that social networks may reveal patterns of prestige (De Nooy, 2003: 320). The hierarchical relations that define a field can be assumed to "create historical conditions for social networks to emerge as the objective form of relational structure" (Singh, 2016: 128).

In what follows I rely on SNA as a supplementary tool for empirical field analysis (De Nooy, 2003). This chapter illustrates a Bourdieusian approach to SNA by mapping a specific form of crystalized action (Sterne, 2003) – "likes" – between the official and public accounts of cultural institutions on Facebook. Rather than studying social structures (the dimensions retrieved from MCA of respondents' access to capital), the approach visualizes a corpus of "found data" (Bruhn Jensen, 2010: 49) and focuses on patterns of interaction that arguably reflect social structures.

The social magic behind inter-institutional "likes" on social media

To illustrate a Bourdieusian approach to SNA applied to digital interactions, the remainder of this chapter visualizes the network of "likes" (edges) between the official Facebook pages of Swedish cultural institutions (nodes) such as theaters, broadcasting companies, art halls, book fairs, and museums. Contrary to MCA-oriented research that reveals "hidden structures" (Duval, 2018: 519) in fields by teasing out latent dimensions from variables measuring agents' access to capitals, focus is here put on the practices that stem from and thus reflect social structures. We turn, in other words, to how fields are enacted and reproduced in practice (De Nooy, 2003). Empirical focus is put on how representatives, or "spokespersons", of cultural institutions manage public Facebook profiles in terms of what other public pages they deem worthy of a "like". We remind ourselves that the "game" of a field is a game over who is recognized as a legitimate player in the field (Hovden, 2012).

Following Bourdieu's (1991b) understanding of social interaction, the following analysis rests on the assumption that the person delegated to manage an organization's official Facebook page is the "legitimated spokesperson, that 'imposter endowed with the skeptron,' [who has been] given control over the process of representation" (Everett, 2002: 68). It is crucial to realize, then, that a "spokesperson" managing an official Facebook page does not act in a social vacuum. When the spokespersons decide which other Facebook pages the institution they represent should "like", they have "the whole social order behind them" (Bourdieu, 1991b: 74). This highlights the Bourdieusian approach to SNA, where interactions between agents constitute a second-tier order, viewed as the outcomes or performances of the logics that pertain to the structure of the field in question. The patterns of outgoing and ingoing "likes" between cultural institutions studied by crawling a digital network are "naturally occurring" (Bail, 2014), crystalized acts of recognition (Sterne, 2003) that capture the ways in which a field is performed. We thus approach transactions of "likes" between the official Facebook pages of cultural institutions as exchanges of recognition that may provide clues about the contours of a social field in terms of who is recognized as a legitimate player in the field.

According to this logic, a spokesperson (be it a communications officer, an intern, or someone else) who manages the official Facebook page of, for instance, the Royal Dramatic Theatre in Stockholm, which is the empirical starting point in this chapter, can be expected to act in accordance with a doxa that sets the imaginative horizon on what a representative of the institution can and cannot do. Like practice in any other field (Bourdieu, 2000), the managing of an institutional Facebook page can be viewed as the extension of a socially shaped habitus that acts in relation to the game that is played in the given field. We start, thus, from the field-theoretical presupposition of a social magic in the tendency of "spokespersons" to embody and perform a social history, making it so that they reproduce the field in their (digital) actions. What takes place thus is "the delegation by virtue of which an individual – king, priest or spokesperson – is mandated to speak and act on behalf of a group, thus constituted in him and by him" (Bourdieu, 1991b: 75). By deciding which other institutions to "like" on social media, spokespersons perform the field, and the digital traces of such performances can be studied to trace the contours of fields and their outer limits.

The field of cultural production in action

The present analysis relied on the Netvizz-application (a free-to-use application that was part of the Facebook app directory, which allowed extracting data from different Facebook functions [Rieder, 2013]) to generate a two-step network of the "likes" between Facebook pages surrounding the official Facebook page of the Royal Dramatic Theatre. Founded in 1788 by King Gustav III (who also initiated the Swedish Academy in 1786) and renovated into its art nouveau style by architect Fredrik Liljekvist, the Royal Dramatic Theatre stood finished as the epitome of institutionalized Swedish cultural life in Nybroplan, Stockholm, in 1908. If there is such a thing as a relatively autonomous field of cultural production (see Bourdieu, 2000) in Sweden, it is relatively safe to assume that the Royal Dramatic Theatre would occupy an established position in that field.

Only official (or "public") pages were included in the crawl. This exercise captured all pages "liked" by the Royal Dramatic Theatre, and all the pages that have been "liked" by those pages. Compared to its "private" counterpart, the "like" of an official Facebook page is more durable since it is not attached to a specific post appearing for a moment in an ever-changing feed; rather, it sticks to the given page (in the "'liked' by this page" section). Furthermore, the problem identified regarding the multiplicity of meanings imbued in the "like" button for the individual and personal use of Facebook – that a "like" can be ironic and signal many other things other than recognition (Baym, 2013; Gerlitz & Helmond, 2013) – is arguably not as much of an issue when it comes to the official pages of institutions. In contrast to the individual social media user, the spokesperson embodies the institution when acting in its place in the online environment. The crawl was conducted in November 2016 and generated a total of 1,214 nodes (Facebook pages) and 8,934 edges (connections, in the form of "likes", between the pages). While the data collected from the crawl hardly counts as "big data" (in terms of its volume), it is exhaustive in the sense that N equals all interactions taking place in the two-step network (cf. Kitchin, 2014). As such it allows getting an initial grasp of the contours and outer limits of the Swedish field of cultural production. Using the open-source software for data visualization Gephi, Figure 6.1 visualizes the result of the crawl of the Royal Dramatic Theatre's official Facebook page and maps all the pages that it has "liked" and the pages that have been "liked" by those other pages. In this figure, the level of ingoing "likes" (in-degree) determines the size of the nodes. This suggests that the biggest nodes are the most recognized players in the field. We see, for example, that the public service broadcaster Swedish Radio, The House of Culture/The City Theatre (Kulturhuset/Stadsteatern), and The Music Aid (Musikhjälpen) constitute some of the central nodes in the network. The arrows represent "likes": an arrow bent clockwise indicates an outgoing "like", whereas a counter-clockwise arrow represents an ingoing "like".

Bourdieu argued that modernity is a process of differentiation that leads to the formation of distinct social fields (Chapter 5) and that the social space is divided between "culture and money" (Bourdieu, 2000). Figure 6.1 captures the contours of the Swedish field of cultural production. The network of "likes" exchanged between cultural institutions thus represents an economy of recognition wherein institutions exclusively recognize other institutions engaging with culture in some way or other. Based on this initial observation, we gain support regarding the existence of a field of culture as a distinct and relatively autonomous social field (Bourdieu, 2000) in contemporary Swedish society. Given that the interactions (transactions of "likes") between the cultural institutions' public pages are exhaustive (for the institutions active on Facebook at the time), we may further suggest that Figure 6.1 captures the main traces of the Swedish field of cultural production anno 2016.

Using the modularity class algorithm (see Blondel et al., 2008), eight distinct clusters of nodes can be identified. This maneuver helps identify the traces of various sub-fields within the broader field of cultural production. Here, it is possible to identify a distinct literary field composed mainly of publishers, book fairs, and libraries. The network also indicates the existence of two fields of media production: the field of television production and the field of radio production. Both these manifestations of fields of media production are highly skewed toward institutions within the public service sector. Commercial broadcasters are generally not recognized by the spokespersons of institutions and organizations in the field of cultural production. This suggests that public service broadcasters are not only included but also recognized as legitimate actors in the wider field of cultural production (for instance, Swedish Radio's public page is the node with the highest number [101] of in-going "likes" in the network) (cf. Bolin, 2014). The previous chapter showed that in the broader field of television production, public service occupies a consecrated and relatively autonomous position. The strong public service character of these two fields of media production, indicated in Figure 6.1, lend support to the notion that public service broadcasting might constitute a field in its

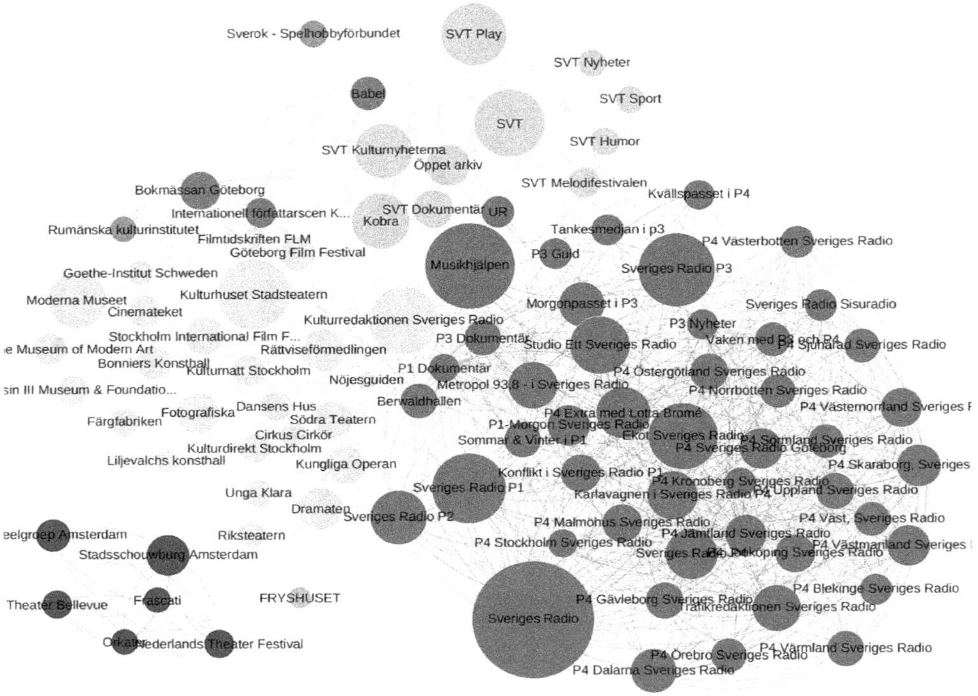

Figure 6.1 The Swedish field of cultural production "in action" (Lindell, 2017: 7)

Note: Visualization of the network surrounding the Royal Dramatic Theatre's (Dramaten) official Facebook page using Gephi and the Force Atlas 2 layout. The grayscale identifies communities within the network based on modular class calculation (.67). Sizes of nodes are based on the number of in-degree of connections. Pages with less than 20 likes have been excluded. The figure has appeared in Lindell (2017: 7).

own right. Additionally, the SNA reveals the traces of a field of institutional-ized fine arts. The ballets, art halls, museums, theaters, and operas share an internal economy of mutual recognition. This sub-field, furthermore, connects to parts of the European field of culture. The network additionally reveals a sub-field of gaming culture comprised of institutions and associations revolv-ing around roleplaying, cosplaying, and digital gaming. Lastly, we find clues about the existence of a hybrid sub-field comprised of associations directed at youth culture (including Fryshuset high school, the anti-bullying organization Friends, as well as UNHCR).

There is undoubtably much more to uncover in the present SNA, and more analyses to be made in regard to the density of the network and its sub-networks and the details on the directionality of the edges ("likes"). The overview pro-vided by the network analysis invites qualitative inquiries into the sub-fields identified. SNA helps reveal the traces of social fields as fields-in-action, but field theory prompts us to approach fields ethnographically. Ethnographic studies into these fields serve a double purpose. On the one hand, interviews with spokespersons managing official social media accounts can shed light on how habitus promotes action in these fields. On the other hand, interviews also help understand what field-specific capitals are active in the field. Fol-lowing such analysis, it would be possible to use surveys to unearth the distri-bution of capitals and to identify the social structures of the field with MCA. This would move the analysis from interactions (field-in-action) to relations between objective properties (field-as-such). Despite the fact that the present Bourdieusian approach to SNA can be supplemented on various counts, it nonetheless suggests that there exists a distinct field of cultural production in Sweden, and that it is maintained by the exchange of recognition between players in the field (cf. Bottero & Crossley, 2011). Where the exchange of recognition stops, the field is likely to cease to have an effect (Bourdieu & Wacquant, 1992). We furthermore get clues about the various sub-fields that exist in the broader field of cultural production. Both of these endeavors – the task of establishing the existence of social fields, and identifying their outer limits – are notoriously difficult (Bail, 2014), and this is a crucial area where the study of networks of interaction in digital data can supplement field theory.

Conclusion

Despite Bourdieu's rejection of network analysis, I have, in line with De Nooy (2003), Singh (2016), Romele and Rodighiero (2020) and others, argued that SNA can supplement field theory. The argument regarding the existence of a field is often made a priori (Bail, 2014). This chapter has argued that there is value in attempting to empirically establish the existence of a field by study-ing its traces in online environments. This would, in Emirbayer's (1997: 304) words, replace Bourdieu's "nominalist" strategy with a "realist" approach to the task of identifying fields. The transactions studied via the network crawl are "naturally occurring" (Bail, 2014) as crystalized acts of recognition (cf. Sterne, 2003) in the online environment. SNA applied to digital transactions offers a way to identify traces of social fields empirically by mapping the totality of transactions of recognition. Additionally, the outer limits of a field are rarely the topic of empirical inquiry. Bourdieu argued that "the limits of the field are situated at the point where the effects of the field cease" (Bourdieu & Wacquant, 1992: 100). SNA applied to interactions among players, in toto, allows identifying where the recognition of legitimate players ceases. As such, the economy of recognition unearthed via the SNA of institutions' exchanges of "likes" produces a relatively rare insight into the amplitude of the field of cultural production. It must be stressed, however, that boundaries and the struggles of inclusion/exclusion are at stake in fields, and thus prone to change over time. We are thus dealing here with a snap-shot of the field-in-action at a given point in time. Furthermore, the present empirical case study of cultural institutions constitutes but one example of how SNA can be incorporated into the broader aims of field theory. There are other networks and types of relations that can be studied in order to understand how fields are performed in digital milieus, and to scrutinize social agents' lifestyles (see, e.g., Sivertsen, 2023). Needless to say, there are also other online platforms from which data can be collected and analyzed for these purposes.

If MCA, with its focus on attributes and properties, identifies the social structures of fields, SNA shifts our focus to practices and how fields are performed (Bottero & Crossley, 2011). Identifying the existence and contours of social fields through the network analysis of automated digital data should not, however, be viewed in a positivistic light where the step of "constructing the object of study" (Bourdieu, 1991a) is skipped. There are dangers in relying on opaque data from private enterprises (e.g., Facebook, X, Instagram, and YouTube). Baym (2013), Lomborg and Bechmann (2014), Hargittai (2015), and others have pointed out that data generated via digital methods oftentimes suffer from sampling issues (indeed, inclusion in the dataset requires membership on a given platform) and bots or trolls that generate "fake" data. Additionally, the black-boxed nature of the (privately owned) platforms from which researchers scrape data hardly helps in terms of transparency, and researchers have to adapt to ever-changing policies when it comes to what data is accessible to external stakeholders, and through which applications and methods. It is thus worth recapitulating Bourdieu's (1991a) insistence that a researcher has to be in command of constructing the object in order to avoid reproducing common-sensical understandings, or in our case the biases in a given platform. Constructing the object of study entails arriving at ethnographic understandings of a given field and surveying its properties to uncover its structures with MCA. Given the deep ethnographic understanding required to "construct" and study a social field, it is unfair to castigate Bourdieu and cultural sociology for simply "assuming" the existence of fields, and there are dangers in thinking that big data analysis would solve all our methodological challenges. Having said this, the sheer scale of data existing in the digital realm helps in identifying discursive fields and locating their outer contours and relationships to other fields (Bail, 2014).

This chapter has suggested that SNA combined with field theory promotes an important focus on how fields manifest in patterns of communication, a focus that should appeal to media and communication scholars. Alongside important discussions on the agency (and habitus) of algorithms and digital media (Romele & Rodighiero, 2020; Airoldi, 2022), field theory opens up for a range of empirical studies where digital data can be analyzed to understand taste, lifestyles, and the crystalized traces of social microcosms.

References

Airoldi, M. (2022). *Machine habitus: Toward a sociology of algorithms*. Cambridge: Polity.

Anheier, H. K., Gerhards, J., & Romo, F. P. (1995). Forms of capital and social structure of fields: Examining Bourdieu's social topography. *American Journal of Sociology*, *100*, 859–903.

Bail, C. A. (2014). The cultural environment: Measuring culture with big data. *Theory & Society*, *43*, 465–482.

Baym, N. K. (2013). Data not seen: The uses and shortcomings of social media metrics. *First Monday*, *18*(10), doi:10.5210/fm.v18i10.4873.

Blondel, V. D., Guillaume, J.-L., Lambiotte, R., & Lefebvre, E. (2008). Fast unfolding communities in large networks. *Journal of Statistical Mechanics* 1–12. doi:10.1088/1742–5468/2008/10/P10008.

Bolin, G. (2014). Television journalism, politics, and entertainment: Power and autonomy in the field of television journalism. *Television & New Media*, *15*(4), 336–49.

Bottero, W., & Crossley, N. (2011). Worlds, fields and networks: Becker, Bourdieu and the structures of social relations. *Cultural Sociology*, *5*(1), 99–119.

Bourdieu, P. (1991a). Meanwhile, I have come to know all the diseases of sociological understanding. In P. Bourdieu, J.-C. Chamboredon, & J.-C. Passeron (Eds.), *The craft of sociology: Epistemological preliminaries* (pp. 247–259). Berlin, New York: Walter de Gruyter.

Bourdieu, P. (1991b). *Language and symbolic power*. Cambridge: Polity.

Bourdieu, P. (2000). *Konstens regler: Det litterära fältets uppkomst och struktur* [The rules of art: Genesis and structure of the literary field]. Stockholm: Brutus Östlings Bokförlag.

Bourdieu, P., & Wacquant, L. (1992). *An invitation to reflexive sociology*. Cambridge: Polity.

Bruhn Jensen, K. (2010). New media, old methods – Internet methodologies and the online/offline divide. In R. Burnett, C. Consalvo, & C. Ess (Eds.), *The handbook of internet studies* (pp. 43–58). Chichester: Wiley Blackwell.

Burrows, R., & Savage, M. (2014). After the crisis? Big data and the methodological challenges of empirical sociology. *Big Data & Society*, *1*(1), 2053951714540280.

Couldry, N., & Mejias, U. A. (2019). Data colonialism: Rethinking big data's relation to the contemporary subject. *Television & New Media*, *20*(4), 336–349.

De Nooy, W. (2003). Fields and networks: Correspondence analysis and social network analysis in the framework of field theory. *Poetics, 31*(5), 305–327.

Duval, J. (2018). Correspondence analysis and Bourdieu's use of statistics: Using correspondence analysis within field theory. In T. Medvetz & J. J. Sallaz (Eds.), *The Oxford handbook of Pierre Bourdieu* (pp. 512–527). Oxford: Oxford University Press.

Elgendy, N., & Elragal, A. (2014). Big data analytics: A literature review paper. In *Advances in data mining. Applications and theoretical aspects: 14th industrial conference, ICDM 2014, St. Petersburg, Russia, July 16–20, 2014. Proceedings 14* (pp. 214–227). Springer International Publishing.

Emirbayer, M. (1997). Manifesto for a relational sociology. *American Journal of Sociology, 103*(2), 281–317.

Everett, J. (2002). Organizational research and the praxeology of Pierre Bourdieu. *Organizational Research Methods, 5*(1), 56–80.

Gaw, F. (2022). Algorithmic logics and the construction of cultural taste of the Netflix recommender system. *Media, Culture & Society, 44*(4), 706–725.

Gerlitz, C., & Helmond, A. (2013). The like economy: Social buttons and the data-intensive web. *New Media & Society, 15*(8), 1348–1365.

Hargittai, E. (2015). Is bigger always better? Potential biases of big data derived from social network sites. *AAPSS, 659*(1), 63–76.

Hovden, J.-F. (2012). A journalistic cosmology: A sketch of some social and mental structures of the Norwegian journalistic field. *Nordicom Review, 33*(2), 57–76.

Ignatow, G., & Robinson, L. (2017). Pierre Bourdieu: Theorizing the digital. *Information, Communication & Society, 20*(7), 950–966.

Kennedy, H., Poell, T., & Van Dijck, J. (2015). Data and agency. *Big Data & Society, 2*(2), 1–7.

Kitchin, R. (2014). Big data, new epistemologies and paradigm shifts. *Big Data & Society, 1*(1), 2053951714528481.

Lindell, J. (2017). Bringing field theory to social media, and vice-versa: Network-crawling an economy of recognition on Facebook. *Social Media + Society, 3*(4), 2056305117735752.

Lindell, J. (2018). *Distinction* recapped: Digital news repertoires in the class structure. *New Media & Society, 20*(8), 3029–3049.

Lomborg, S., & Bechmann, A. (2014). Using APIs for data collection on social media. *The Information Society, 30*(4), 256–265.

Lundahl, O. (2022). Algorithmic meta-capital: Bourdieusian analysis of social power through algorithms in media consumption. *Information, Communication & Society, 25*(10), 1440–1455.

Mejias, U. A. (2010). The limits of networks as models for organizing the social. *New Media & Society, 12*(4), 603–617.

Mohr, J. W. (2013). Bourdieu's relational method in theory and in practice: From fields and capitals to networks and institutions (and back again). In F. Dépelteau & C. Powell (Eds.), *Applying relational sociology: Relations, networks, and society* (pp. 101–135). New York: Palgrave Macmillan US.

Mohr, J. W., Bail, C. A., Frye, M., Lena, J. C., Lizardo, O., McDonnell, T. E., Mische, A., Tavory, I., Wherry, F. F. (2020). *Measuring culture*. New York: Columbia University Press.

Otte, E., & Rousseau, R. (2002). Social network analysis: A powerful strategy, also for the information sciences. *Journal of Information Science, 28*(6), 441–453.

Rieder, B. (2013). Studying Facebook via data extraction: The Netvizz application. *Proceedings of the 5th Annual ACM Web Science Conference* (pp. 346–355).

Romele, A., & Rodighiero, D. (2020). Digital habitus or personalization without personality. *Journal of Philosophical Studies, 13*(37), 98–126.

Sadowski, J. (2019). When data is capital: Datafication, accumulation, and extraction. *Big Data & Society, 6*(1), 2053951718820549.

Scott, J. (2012). *What is social network analysis?* New York: Bloomsbury Academic.

Segre, S. (2004). A Durkheimian network theory. *Journal of Classical Sociology, 4*(2), 215–235.

Singh, S. (2016). What is relational structure? Introducing history to the debates on the relation between fields and social networks. *Sociological Theory, 34*(2), 128–150.

Sivertsen, M. (2023). *Stratified publics: A sociological study of inequality in citizenship, media, and public formation in the digital era.* [Doctoral Dissertation, Roskilde University].

Solaroli, M. (2016). The rules of a middle-brow art: Digital production and cultural consecration in the global field of professional photojournalism. *Poetics, 59*, 50–66.

Sterne, J. (2003). Bourdieu, technique and technology. *Cultural Studies, 17*(3–4), 367–389.

Zuboff, S. (2015). Big other: surveillance capitalism and the prospects of an information civilization. *Journal of Information Technology, 30*(1), 75–89.

7   Summary and conclusion

Summary

While Bourdieu's concepts are widely used in many corners in the field of media and communication studies, his research program is seldom fleshed out in full. Attempts to put his program to use in the construction and design of empirical studies in our field are rare (Chapter 1). This was the gap that the present book set out to fill. Accordingly, the aim was to answer the question of what "Bourdieusian media studies" entails: which are the main Bourdieusian concepts, what do they mean, and, importantly, what do they imply in terms of conducting empirical research in media and communication studies? By illustrating Bourdieusian media studies not only conceptually but also empirically, the ambition has been to say something meaningful about the relationship between social inequality and media use, the social dynamics of contemporary media and cultural production, as well as networks of interaction on digital media.

Adding to the body of previous introductions to Bourdieu's field theory, Chapter 2 focused primarily on the notions of field, capital, and habitus and anchored these in relation to research interests within media and communication studies. In addressing the misalignment between theory and empirical work in previous Bourdieu-inspired media and communication scholarship, Chapter 3 turned to multiple correspondence analysis (MCA) and explained how the epistemological principles of field theory can be translated into empirical work. The chapter clarified the various approaches to the empirical object (the reciprocal approach and the social space/field approach) and spelled out the steps taken when conducting Bourdieusian research. MCA was applied to study the structure of the contemporary Swedish social space. Findings suggested that the principles of capital volume and capital composition were reflected in the main axes of the space. Inspired in large parts by Bourdieu's (1984) *Distinction*, Chapter 4 studied the distribution of media practices in the social space. Analyses showed how news consumption, smartphone use, and television preferences correspond to specific positions in the multidimensional space of subordination and domination (the social space).

DOI: 10.4324/9781003364245-7

The chapter highlighted both clear-cut stratification of media practice (consumption of "quality news") and less straightforward patterns (smartphone uses), and argued for supplementing the strict focus on the homology thesis and (class) habitus with analyses on, for example, gender, age, and ethnicity. Leaning mainly on *The Rules of Art* (Bourdieu, 1996) and a more recent attempt to operationalize field theory (Fligstein & McAdam, 2012), Chapter 5 focused on using MCA to study fields revolving around the production (the field of television production) and analysis (the field of media and communication studies) of media. Findings highlighted that fields tend to be structured by the level of consecration and volumes of field-specific capital on the one hand, and differences in ideologies of practice on the other (e.g., "art for art's sake" vs. mass production in the literary field, or public service broadcasting vs. commercial production in the field of television production). Digitalization was highlighted as an exogenous force in regard to institutionalized cultural production, as fields become both more homogenous and heteronomous in relation to the global attention economy. Chapter 6 moved beyond MCA and discussed how data scraped off of online platforms and social network analysis (SNA) may supplement MCA-oriented research in terms of identifying traces of social fields and investigating their outer limits.

Conclusion: Bourdieusian media studies – a research program

> I offer a programme for other empirical analyses conducted in situations different from the one I've studied.
>
> (Bourdieu, 1991: 255)

Bourdieusian media studies is a media sociological research program dedicated first and foremost to the study of media use and the production of culture within hierarchized social contexts (Benson, 1999; Lindell, 2015). It is a program that is essentially non-media-centric, that puts focus on power relations and symbolic domination. It takes into account both "objective" structures (such as the distribution of capital) and "subjective" orientations (such as lifestyles and position-takings). The main concepts that operationalize "social context" and "objective structures" are social space on the one hand and field on the other. These concepts differ in respect to the scale of the inquiry. The former deals primarily with society at large (but also with regions or cities [e.g., Prieur et al., 2008]), whereas the latter focuses on distinct mezzo-level social microcosms. The concept of habitus captures the socially shaped ways in which social agents apprehend and move about in the world, and as such it allows focusing on how subjective dimensions of social life relate to social structures. The Bourdieusian approach promotes the open-ended and empirical study of relations between agents and objective properties, or between various cultural goods (in the space of lifestyles). Throughout the book these tendencies, which describe the relative stability of social structures and the persistence of social inequality in terms of how social groups make sense of various media, were uncovered with MCA. Other methods supplement MCA on different counts – ethnography helps gaining a preliminary understanding of a field before collecting data for MCA, qualitative interviews promote rich accounts of subjective position-takings, content analysis can be crucial in systematizing prosopographic data, and network analyses of data scraped from online platforms can reveal traces of social fields and map their reach. MCA nonetheless remains the main method in Bourdieusian media studies since it is a "technique that 'thinks' in terms of relationships, as I try to do with the idea of the field" (Bourdieu, 1991: 254).

Twenty-five years ago, Rodney Benson presented Bourdieu's field theory as a "new paradigm for media studies" (1999: 463). Like other, more established, research traditions in media and communication studies, including critical discourse analysis, cultural studies, framing theory, cultivation theory, and uses and gratifications research, Bourdieusian media studies comprises a set of interrelated theoretical concepts and a corresponding method with which to put concepts to use in empirical work. Like other research programs, then, Bourdieusian media studies is endowed with what we may, with Lakatos (1999), refer to as a "hard core" – an overarching and stable theory of the social world and an auxiliary relational methodology (see Chapters 2 and 3). Yet, in media and communication studies, the Bourdieusian approach has not fully been realized as a research program. One could say that the numerous studies in our field that apply one concept or facet of field theory orbit the "protective belt" (Lakatos, 1999) of the core of field theory, where isolated fragments of the theory are evaluated, refuted, or re-worked. The main contribution of this book is its attempt at teasing out the "hard core" of field theory for media and communication scholars. By uncovering the main epistemological principles and their consequences for empirical research, without pretending to cover Bourdieu's oeuvre in its entirety, I hope to have shown that scholars and students of media and communication have much to gain from a holistic approach to field theory. With the empirical studies of this book, I wish to have illustrated that Bourdieusian media studies can be put to use to answer important questions in media and communications, including how social agents maneuver in the digital media landscape, the social conditions of media and cultural production, and the broader sociological dynamics pertaining to social interactions on digital platforms.

References

Benson, R. (1999). Field theory in comparative context: A new paradigm for media studies. *Theory and Society, 28*(3), 463–498.

Bourdieu, P. (1984). *Distinction: A social critique of the judgement of taste.* New York: Routledge.

Bourdieu, P. (1991). Meanwhile, I have come to know all the diseases of sociological understanding. In P. Bourdieu, J.-C. Chamboredon, & J.-C. Passeron (Eds.), *The craft of sociology: Epistemological preliminaries* (pp. 247–259). Berlin, New York: Walter de Gruyter.

Bourdieu, P. (1996). *The rules of art: Genesis and structure of the literary field.* Cambridge: Polity.

Fligstein, N., & McAdam, D. (2012). *A theory of fields.* Oxford: Oxford University Press.

Lakatos, I. (1999). *The methodology of scientific research programmes.* Cambridge: Cambridge University Press.

Lindell, J. (2015). Bourdieusian media studies: Returning social theory to old and new media. *Distinktion: Scandinavian Journal of Social Theory, 16*(3), 362–377.

Prieur, A., Rosenlund, L., & Skjott-Larsen, J. (2008). Cultural capital today: A case study from Denmark. *Poetics, 36*(1), 45–71.

Index

For Product Safety Concerns and Information please contact our EU
representative GPSR@taylorandfrancis.com
Taylor & Francis Verlag GmbH, Kaufingerstraße 24, 80331 München, Germany

www.ingramcontent.com/pod-product-compliance
Lightning Source LLC
Chambersburg PA
CBHW061748270326
41928CB00011B/2423